PETALS AND BLOOD

*Stories, Dharma & Poems
of Ecstasy, Awakening & Annihilation*

Gavin Harrison

Author of *In the Lap of the Buddha*

Pau Press

This book is lovingly dedicated to:

My teachers
Joseph Goldstein
Adyashanti
Mukti

My parents
Adelaide and Ronald Harrison
and
my brother
Craig James Harrison

The women, men and children
of
the *Woza Moya Project*
and
the *Group of Hope*
in South Africa

and
The People of Hawai'i

Proceeds from the sale of this book will benefit
the *Woza Moya Project* and the *Group of Hope.*

OTHER WORKS BY GAVIN HARRISON

In the Lap of the Buddha
(Shambhala Publications, 1994)

Additional published writings at gavinharrison.net.

Library of Congress Cataloging-in-Publication Data
Petals and Blood: Stories, Dharma and Poems of Ecstasy,
Awakening and Annihilation. / Gavin Harrison.
xiv, 122 p., |c22.9 cm.
ISBN 978-0-9891998-1-0
1.poetry 2. mysticism 3. Buddhism 4. spirituality
2013905500

First printing October 2013

Printed in China on partially recycled paper at a facility in
compliance with child labor laws and fair wage requirements.

To order copies of this book, visit petalsandblood.com.

ACKNOWLEDGMENTS

Layout, Graphics and Visuals

Every page of this book evidences the great heart and talent of *Tim Dubitsky*. Our collaboration has been among the great blessings of my life.

Editing and Proofreading

There must be a special place in heaven for editors and proofreaders. Thank you all:

Kim Criswell—Editor, Copy Editor and *Final Proofreading*
Richard Bodien—Initial Editor
and
Carol Salisbury Culbertson, Eila Algood, Craig Harrison, Fred Hanson, Holly Algood, Kevin McVeigh, Kim Rosen, Matilda Tompson, Nancy Owen Barton and Shirley Stoffer.

Photographers

I am honored and thankful that my poems now rest within the glorious photography of:

Carlos Eyles, Catherine Anderson, Therese Cooper and Wendy Wagner.

Friends of *Petals and Blood*

Heartfelt gratitude to the innumerable friends and cheerleaders who have buoyed the birthing of this book. They include:

Beth Thoma Robinson , Barbara Gates, Brian O'Donnell, Carol Wilson, Cheyenne Maloney, Frederick Kennedy, Georgina Hamilton, Jack Boyle, Jan Roberts, Jay Williams, Jatta Tapio, Joey Bradley, Karen Rosen, Keith Nealy, Keith Wallis, Kim Rosen, Lila Wheeler, Linda Scott, Michael Reardon, Nancy Taylor, Trudy Goodman and all those above.

TABLE OF CONTENTS

FOREWORD

I have known Gavin Harrison as a student, friend and colleague since 1981 and although I have spent many hours over all these years in intimate conversations with him, his extraordinary new book *Petals and Blood: Stories, Dharma and Poems of Ecstasy, Awakening And Annihilation* reveals even more of his personal story. Gavin's early years in South Africa, his time in Iran and the United States, and his return visits to South Africa are all deeply imprinted upon his life journey. It is a journey of spiritual discovery that finds the beauty of life in the depths of his struggles with illness, in the often-impoverished conditions of black South Africans, and in the profound depths of his spiritual unfolding. The fierceness of Gavin's commitment to the Truth has been the spark that has ignited the vast compassion of his heart.

It is rare to find a book in which the intimacy of the prose, the inspiration of the poetry and the striking beauty of the photographs interweave into such a unified whole. Of course, that wholeness describes Gavin himself, and *Petals and Blood* is a fitting testament to his amazing life. It is a book to savor in quiet hours, letting his personal story open your heart; his poetry, and that of the great masters Rumi and Hafiz, inspire new depths of understanding and love; and the beautiful imagery of the photographs provide a refuge of silence, peace and repose.

I'm grateful that Gavin has shared his life in this way.

Joseph Goldstein
Barre, MA
September 15, 2012

INTRODUCTION

POEMS AND STORIES

The poems within this book have been offered at public gatherings in Hawai'i and South Africa. Afterwards, there is usually a community meal where new and old friends, spiritual seekers and lovers of poetry can connect and be together before leaving. Always there is laughter and a lot of noise! The poems have also been offered into the quietude of long meditation retreats, where they move easily upon landscapes of contemplation and stillness.

The seven chapters of poetry included in this book follow an arc that has evolved at these gatherings, beginning with poems of **INVOCATION**, a call to sacred space and courage. Poems of **LONGING** move into the fortifying aspects of the spiritual journey, including devotion, surrender, yearning and a love of Truth.

FIRE poems are a direct engagement of our humanity. They include grappling with emotions, thoughts, busyness, resistance, and our relationship with experiences, frustration and the birthing of a capacity to allow things to be as they are. We are invited into the field of interconnectedness, support and communion with others, near and far, with poems of **TOGETHERNESS**.

"Bridge to Nowhere" transitions us into an exploration of the **INDESCRIBABLE**, encompassing the relative and absolute aspects of reality, the shortcomings and fallibility of language, the birth of creativity and the recognition of our True Nature.

With **LOVE** we enter the heart's domain, exploring the blossoming of True Love and its expression in the world. **GRATITUDE** completes the arc with poems of fruition, ecstasy, thankfulness and amazement, pointing towards the limitless, impersonal, always-and-already-given, Awake Essence of who we are and the fundamental Nature of Existence itself.

In the *Lap of the Buddha* (Shambhala Publications, 1994). was an endeavor to present the fundamental teachings of the Buddha in an intimate and frank way, embracing issues not yet fully within the discourse of Buddhism at the time—including sexual abuse, AIDS and homosexuality. *Petals and Blood* relentlessly points towards a freedom larger than any issue could ever be. Each chapter begins with personal stories, anecdotes and reflections related to the theme of that chapter's poems.

In Hawai'i the tradition of "talk-story" is deeply rooted in the ancient ways. When we gather at the feet of the well-traveled and the elderly and listen without agenda, all ears and heart, we can find their stories instructive, perhaps even pointing to the depths of who we are and the very Nature of Existence. Every human story carries intimations of the Infinite, if we are undistracted by details. The stories within *Petals and Blood* celebrate the human and fallible ground from which these poems have emerged and an awakening nourished by that same ground. Because these stories are not sequential, a brief synopsis of my life may be helpful.

I was born in Johannesburg, South Africa, in 1950. When I was ten years old I was sent to boarding school in Kimberly, 300 miles away from home. After graduating high school in 1967 and completing a year of conscripted military service, I began studies at The University of the Witwatersrand in Johannesburg, graduating as a chartered accountant in 1973. In 1974 I left South Africa with my partner of three years. He and I traveled in Europe and eventually settled in Iran. Our relationship ended in 1978 and I moved to New York City. On a

return visit to South Africa in 1981, I met Joseph Goldstein at my first meditation retreat and lived at the Buddhist Retreat Centre in KwaZulu-Natal for a year afterwards.

Soon after my return to the USA in 1982, I began a yearlong monastic commitment. A few days before entering the monastery, I was unknowingly infected with the HIV virus. After leaving the order, I settled in Western Massachusetts, reconnected with Joseph Goldstein and began attending annual three-month meditation retreats at the Insight Meditation Society, outside Barre, Massachusetts. I was diagnosed HIV-positive in July 1989. In 1998 I settled in Hawai'i.

HAFIZ, RUMI AND SUFISM

The intersection of my life with the Sufi poets Hafiz and Rumi turned my world upside down. Their ecstatic poems are thunderbolts striking the depths of who I really am, challenging me to settle for nothing less than unbridled liberation, here and now. Their intoxication with The Divine leaves me drunk with longing and devotion. They demand I encounter all that inhibits the flourishing of my wild and irrepressible heart. They evidence the Sacred Union that is the birthright of us all. "The Entirety and the Particular" and "Petals and Blood" are poems of adoration, respect and struggle with these men whom I consider my abiding teachers, mentors and icons of inspiration and possibility.

Both Hafiz and Rumi became disciples of their teachers during an era when Sufi schools abounded. Sufism is the mystical dimension of Islam. Rumi's teacher was Shams al-Din Mohammad of Tabriz. Hafiz was a student of Mohammad Attar of Shiraz. Rumi was likely born in 1207, in present-day Tajikistan, before moving as an infant to Turkey. He died in the autumn of 1273. Information about Hafiz is less definitive. He was probably born in 1320 and died around 1389 in Shiraz where he lived.

In this book I have quoted, with permission, translations of Hafiz by Daniel Ladinsky, and Rumi by Coleman Barks.

MUSIC

At gatherings, my poetry is usually accompanied by live music, a sacred element of each adventure. The poems are interlinked with stories, spontaneous and responsive to the gathering, always weaving a web of invitation, seduction and mischief.

For Rumi, music, poetry and dance were critical ingredients for Awakening. It was from these elements that the practice of the whirling dervishes developed into a ritual form within his Order of the Mevlevi.

The poetry of Hafiz inclines enduringly towards a sensuality of language and imagery. Within the field of his poems, the senses come alive with an intermingling of smell, taste, texture, color and sound. Even when not explicit, enchanting music, bewitching beauty, intoxicating fragrance and delectable savoring are endlessly implied within his poems.

THE BELOVED

There are many words within the great spiritual traditions that point towards The Unnamable. For much of my life I was allergic to the pointers, particularly "God," the white-bearded guy in the sky who hovered over my African childhood with judgment and malevolence.

Hafiz and Rumi changed everything. Their exuberance was mercilessly seditious. Their ecstatic devotion set my heart afire with a fierce longing for The Truth, what the Sufis frequently call My Beloved or The Beloved, as do I now. Love-struck before The Beloved, poetry is my best shot at bringing into words the struggles and blossoming of my grateful heart.

I am frequently asked: *Who is this Beloved that you love so much?* It's an important question that's impossible to answer. The poem "Slippery One" is a playful response. Any attempt to describe The Indescribable is a wild madness. The paragraphs that follow are a humble endeavor to elucidate The Unimaginable. May I fail well, perhaps even eloquently!

My relationship with The Beloved is multifaceted, a jewel with three shifting faces. Through each facet the others are evident.

I had an introduction to The Beloved while a monk at a monastic community in 1982, where early each morning I took ritual refuge in the Triple Gem of Buddhism: refuge in the Buddha, the Dharma and the Sangha.

My refuge in the Buddha was a turning towards that which is already Whole, Awake and Undivided within me, an essential loveliness untouched by circumstance, my Buddha Nature awaiting my arrival. This refuge has evolved into the first facet of my love affair with The Beloved. It is personal, intimate and subjective, as are the poems "Across the Veld" and "No Created Thing".

My refuge in the Dharma, or The Truth, was redolent with devotion and a sense of the enormity before which I bowed in surrender each morning. Here the relationship is objective, carrying a sense of otherness. Poems in conversation with this face of My Beloved include "I Only Have Eyes for You" and "It's Just As Well."

My refuge in the Sangha, or Community, had a reach and inclusiveness that extended way beyond the nuns and monks with whom I lived. This Refuge evokes the unifying expression of my relationship with The Beloved, the interrelatedness of everything and a web of life where isolation and disconnection are impossible. "No Created Thing", "Carnival" and "Petals and Blood" are homages to this face of My Beloved.

THE PHOTOGRAPHS

My prayer is that the beautiful photographs in this book will convey the majesty of the two places that gave birth to these poems: South Africa where I was born, and Hawai'i where I now live. These pages have been graced by the remarkable photography of Wendy Wagner and Carlos Eyles of Hawai'i, and Catherine Anderson and Therese Cooper of South Africa. (See Appendix 5.)

IN CLOSING

In essence, the poetry within this collection is indistinguishable from the spiritual teachings I have offered over the last twenty years. While the vehicle of transmission appears different, both forms carry an enduring invitation to awaken to the very deepest Truth of who we are. To distinguish between that deeper Truth and the ordinary truths of everyday life, I capitalize words pointing towards The Indescribable in my poems and texts.

I am a student of my poems. Sometimes they point to what I don't yet fully recognize within myself or they pull me beyond the edge of what is being revealed. The poems may change and evolve as I memorize and perform them for audiences. No longer rooted as the centerpiece within the story of my life, the poems track an evolution out of the fixated personal, into a largess of Self, way bigger than any story could ever be.

With the annihilation of all I once believed myself to be, the seeker who set out on this journey has not returned.

May the poems, stories and photographs in this book release a fragrance of that which is Sacred, Timeless and Universal. And may you hear the music also.

Gavin Harrison
North Kohala, Big Island of Hawai'i
May 2013

THE POEMS

*Wherever your eyes and arms and heart
can move
Against the earth and sky,
The Beloved has bowed there—
Our Beloved has bowed there knowing
You were coming.*

—*Hafiz*

Invocation

The poems in this book have been offered in many beautiful and sacred places, including a bamboo building in Hawai'i enveloped by roaring winds and a wild ocean; an old rock barn in South Africa, alive and on fire with candles and proteas harvested from the surrounding mountainsides; and a Hawaiian homestead, rich with history and orchids, anthuriums and heliconias.

Sacred space helps consecrate that which is True, Whole and Sacred within us. Gathering in a way that is authentic and human blesses us with the possibility of entering the Fields of the Infinite, where recognition of the depths of who we truly are becomes an immediate possibility. In the Sufi tradition, the Tavern is a metaphor for the everydayness of life, the rough-and-tumble within which we learn about relationships, human fallibility and ourselves. I invoke the image of the Tavern as the context for poetry gatherings. The currency within the Tavern is music, stories, tears and laughter. The mysterious forces of love enter the sacred matrix of our togetherness. It is a wild, rowdy and uninhibited place where every part of us is welcomed and allowed. Neither precious nor sterile, in the Tavern we engage and collide with one another, experiencing the fragility of our humanness. It is messy and unpredictable. We get dirty. Sparks fly. We drink the wine of self-honesty and become drunk upon the

possibility of being deeply free. Within the Tavern we eventually discover a way of being with others and ourselves that is increasingly loving, kind and trustworthy. The anarchy of the Tavern draws us towards a recognition of our True Nature and The Essence of Existence.

In 1990 I shared two deeply impactful experiences with my mother, Adelaide, within the sacred space of the Tavern. We were among two hundred people participating in a weeklong workshop together—fathers, mothers, sisters, brothers and others affected by AIDS. This was a time of death and fear, with no effective drugs and few viable responses to the tragedy.

All of us gathered one evening in an old church in upstate New York. We sat in silence for a great while. Candles flickered. Flowers withered. Suddenly a great scream pierced the quiet and a portal opened for a ferocious upwelling of fear, frustration, disappointment, sadness and outrage. Adelaide was emotionally untethered and uninhibited, bereft beyond describing. I wept for the first time since my diagnosis the year before, grieving friends who had died and fearing my own death.

Eventually the building returned to silence. As we entered the darkness outside, Adelaide reached for my hand.

Each afternoon she participated in a workshop focused upon "Forgiveness." On our final night together, all two hundred of us gathered beside a beautiful lake at sunset. Out of the trees emerged a huge effigy structured out of chicken wire into which the "Forgiveness" participants had pushed pieces of paper, describing things they were willing to forgive, along with pleas for forgiveness for things they had done.

It was a raucous procession. Adelaide led the pilgrimage to the waterside, brandishing a huge flaming torch and screeching at the top of her voice, *Forgive! Forgive! Forgive!* My seventy-year-old mother who had never been to a workshop or therapist in her life was behaving like a wild banshee, surrounded by a frenzy of people who adored her.

At the lake's edge she entered a wilder dimension of madness. Screaming and whirling, she set the effigy aflame.

When the fire calmed and emotions began to settle she walked over to me with tears in her eyes. She took my hand and said, *Please forgive me for not protecting you Gavin, and for sending you to boarding school. I am so sorry.* It was a moment that jumpstarted a deep healing between us.

During the ensuing years, Adelaide and I doggedly addressed all the gnarly threads of our intersected lives. It was a miracle birthed beside still waters, in the dark. We eventually resolved everything. She became my best friend. Our final years together were without complication and saturated with love. Each time we said goodbye, when I left South Africa or she left the United States, it was with a mutual assumption that we might not see one another again.

In our sacred and emotional farewells, we said everything, always acknowledging our love, gratitude and respect for each other. In 2011 we said farewell for the final time in South Africa.

WE ARE
NOT ALONE

We are not alone.

Lovers of mystery and adventure
have already entered
the portals of our togetherness.

From every direction,
mischief and mayhem
are fast approaching.

Half-heartedness,
indifference
and
the commonplace
will find
no friendship here.

Stand wild.

Stand naked,
within this moment.

Fall from the contraction
of your mind
into the cathedral of your heart.

And give yourself
to the otherness
of our time together.

By the end of our adventuring,
you may decide not to make
the return journey,
ever.

Walk on the wild side for a while.

Be here just the way you are.

Human,
real,
authentic.

No pretense.

No pretending.

Cast caution and concern
to the gathering winds.

Step across your thresholds
of safety and hesitation.

Rest.

Relax.

Arrive.

Stop completely!

Unfasten your seatbelt.

Leave your preconceptions,
expectations,
views,
opinions
and
all memory of other poetry
beyond
the threshold of our doorstep.

And be available
to the grace
and the good fortune
already upon its way,
bowing before the possibilities of
this sacred time together.

WELCOME TO THE TAVERN

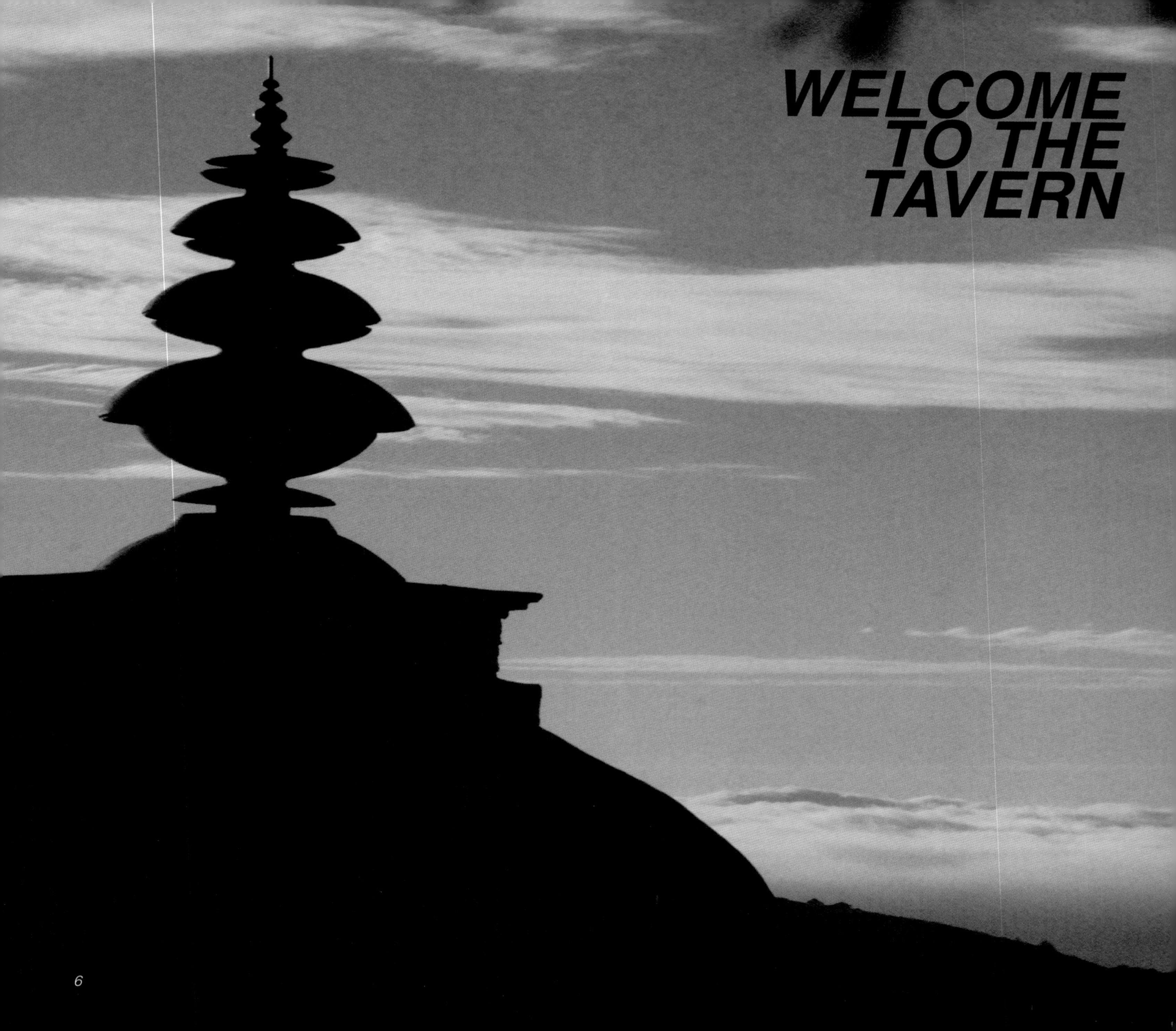

Welcome!

This Tavern is open.

24/7!

365!

The blinds,
torn from the windows.

The curtains,
scattered to the winds.

The glass,
shattered into infinity.

Every door,
wrenched from its hinges.

Are you willing to lose yourself
completely?

This is the price of admission.

Stay awake,
alert,
vigilant.

You never know
from which direction
The Beloved
will have its way with you.

Perhaps we are jumping in puddles
out in the courtyard
or
cruising the neighbors next door.

Join us
if you have the constitution
for nonsense,
stupidity
and irreverence.

Or maybe we are
in one of the upstairs chambers,
making love from the inside out.

Don't be shy.

Our Beloved loves making love
with all of us,
within all our wild disguises.

And you my dear
are a particularly tantalizing
expression of
The Infinite Mystery.

Cut loose!

Catapult your heart
beyond comfort and concern.

And maybe you want
to join us at the bar.

We have been expecting you.

Within this establishment
there are four Holy Sacraments.

We break bread.

We drink wine.

We fall into love.

We dance naked.

The tables
are excellent for this.

Come on my friend,
give us the old razzle-dazzle.

This Tavern is wide open!

Sobriety, unacceptable!

Eat,
pray,
laugh,
dance,
cavort,
love
and disappear completely.

While Our Beloved
accompanies your extinction
upon the ukulele.

THE
COURAGE
OF A LION

*C*hrist wandered the desert,
alone.

The Buddha
sat under the Bodhi Tree,
all by himself.

Are you willing
to stand naked and solitary
before all that inhibits
the fruition of your homecoming?

You are more than ready
for the great adventure
entrusted to you.

For within your heart,
restless and waiting,
is the courage of a lion.

Prowling the prison bars
of its incarceration.

Roaring your song of Homecoming.

Longing for the liberation
of your loveliness once and for all.

It's up to you my friend.

Unwilling to move
to those places that scare you?

You will reside in a fortress of fear
for all time.

Unwilling
to let The Light of Truth illuminate
the hidden corridors of shadow?

Those passageways will receive
your darkening footfalls
forever.

Plunge into the ravine as Jacob* did!

Grapple with God,
innocent,
alone,
unselfconscious,
beside the river of your life.

Enter the darkness.

Discover only light.

Be steadfast in your resolution
and a great roar will accompany you
to the other side!

And you too will be blessed
with the glory of Truth and Love,
as Jacob was,
upon the banks of the Jabbok River*,
beside which you both stand now.

And as the radiance of a new day
dawns around you,
throw yourself to the ground
before the sacred altar of your life.

Feel the Love you are
beginning to flow
like the river beside you.

Move to the genesis
of
your humanity and divinity.

Give yourself to yourself.

Demand
the blessing of your birthright.

Turn towards the Promised Land.

For you are the Light of the World
and
shall be called "Israel" also,
the one who wrestles
with the God of Truth and Love.

*Beside the Jabbok River, Jacob wrestled with,
and finally surrendered to, God. It is where he was
given his new name "Israel, the one who wrestles
with God." (Genesis. 32:22). Jabbok means "a place
of passing over."

Beloved,
I am waiting for You to free me
Into Your Mind
And Infinite Being.
I am pleading in
absolute helplessness
To hear, finally, your Words of Grace:
Fly! Fly into Me!

—*Hafiz*

LONGING

A significant blessing of my life has been the clarification of what is most important to my heart. At long last the inner ducks are in a row now, fortifying my willingness and fueling my longing for union with My Beloved no matter what, every moment of every day.

I yearn for union. The longing of my heart is the journey now. Agonizing discontent arises if my fidelity to what is Real and True wavers. The hunger was always there, focused for much of my life upon objects and experiences of titillation and obsession, always carrying the seeds of suffering and frustration. Since then, every time I follow this thread to its source, I discover that everything I once wanted was fundamentally a longing for My Beloved, an intimacy with The Truth.

Within my heart, I am gratefully and happily married to The One who cannot and will never leave me. Very slowly a shift of allegiance occurred, a gradual movement from the apparently reliable towards a Beloved that promises no security or solid ground, ever. My devotion to The Beloved at last supersedes my need for certainty.

How well I remember my mother's profile as I lay under the covers as she knelt at the foot of my bed. I was four years old. This was the loveliest part of my day as we said our goodnight prayer together, *Gentle Jesus meek and mild, look upon this little child, protect my simplicity, suffer me to come to Thee.* Then she would close the curtains, kiss me goodnight and shut the bedroom door.

If heavy African storm clouds did not hang thick, dark and low across the sky, bright moonlight fell through the bedroom windows for a few wonderful nights every month, summoning me from sleep and drawing me outside again and again. The curtains could not keep the full moon from calling.

In my pajamas I slipped down from the bed and crossed the room to the door. I reached for

---

the handle and slowly pulled it down, careful to make no sound whatsoever. If the crickets outside were noisy, I felt bolder as I slipped into the hallway. I knew when my father was asleep. His snoring reverberated to every corner of the house. If my mother's bed did not creak or groan, it was safe to tiptoe towards the front door. Here I had to be meticulous. Reaching up, I disabled the burglar alarm, a labyrinth of copper wire and passwords. I turned the key, breathless with anticipation.

Through the open doorway I beheld a wonderland outside beckoning me to play. Bright silvery moonbeams held me as I walked along the garden path to the fields of grass below. Every dewdrop sparkled and laughed in the light. Stars twinkled across the heavens and the great, round moon smiled down, anointing me with love. I felt indistinguishable from the magic surrounding me. I was in love, at play in

the happiest place on earth. The magnolia blossoms hovered like clouds upon the branches above my head, the air heavy with their fragrance. Tall snowdrop lilies danced in the moonlight as I lay on the grass and looked up at the stars through their liquid petals. If the great old cactus was in bloom, its long white trumpet flowers reached up towards the heavens, petals sipping moonlight through the night. I ran to every corner of the garden. I danced and spun in the silvery air, always watching for the first intimations of dawn when I returned to bed before my parents awoke, pajamas wet with dew and a heart overflowing with unrestrained and innocent love.

It was a foggy evening in South Africa as I began my bumpy ascent up the mountain in 1981. Although I did not know it at the time, the longing of my heart for The

Beloved drew me towards an adventure that would call into question every part of my life. I was about to begin my first faltering steps upon an ancient path traveled by countless others before me. That my heart and spirit would be wildly ignited by silence and meditation was unthinkable. Winding my way through the undulating countryside of the Valley of a Thousand Hills, past misty Zulu villages and through great forestlands, I drew closer to a way of being that would take me beyond the limited notion of who or what I thought I was.

The Buddhist Retreat Centre hugs a hillside looking into the Ofafa Valley. I stepped out of the car and breathed in the clean, thin air. The South African author Alan Paton called this part of Africa, "a land more beautiful than the singing of it." The rumble of drums rolled up the mountainside. Fires

flickered in the valley below. Mist swirled among the trees outside. Sounds of the African night filled the air and floated through the windows of the meditation hall. A serene face of the Buddha stared at me from the front.

Joseph Goldstein entered and began, *We all are sharing something very special in having the opportunity to be here to look within ourselves in this quiet and secluded setting. It is rare to have a period of time devoted to meditation, to find out about ourselves.*

During the retreat I sensed the possibility of engaging the challenges of my life. Within the simple silence of sitting, walking, eating, listening and resting together, my heart turned towards a teaching, a spiritual practice, and a man who felt utterly trustworthy and dependable.

I
ONLY
HAVE EYES
FOR YOU

I am tired of talking so much.

I cannot get it up
for drama any longer.

I am done with mediocrity
and the commonplace.

Nothing less than Home will do.

This has been a bloody adventure,
and now
I only have eyes for You.

May nothing supersede
this ribald devotion.

Please be patient with me
should the world of fantasies
seduce this heart again.

And indulge my fallibility
if I forage for happiness out there,
lunatic I can be sometimes.

I used to care about what people
thought of me
and
how I looked.

Now I only have eyes for You.

I tried so hard to please everyone
and
preconceive the ingredients
of their happiness.

Now I only have eyes for You.

My efforts to be good,
perfect and homogenized,
were failed to disasters.

Now I only have eyes for You.

I've turned a corner, My Beloved.

It's all about you now.

You are the One!

And may this trail of blood
evidence the flowering
of a trustworthy and humbled heart.

And within Your arms
I am willing
to disappoint and distress
the entire population if necessary,
and
unequivocally,
never betray You,
My Beloved,
ever again.

PRAYER
TO PELE

*T*here was no intimation,
  My Beloved,
of the raging fire
into which my life would fall.

Every part of me carries
the scar tissue of this inferno.

It is a mystery
from which direction
You will erupt
and where
You will have Your way next.

Beloved Pele,
Goddess of Fire,
I cast myself upon
the molten landscape
of
Your benevolence.

I'm willing to be a
child of fire,
forevermore.

This is my humble prayer:

Birth within me
the courage of a firewalker
and
may the flames within this
bloodstream
never deflect me
from my longing for You
nor
fray the edges of my resolve.

Bring heat,
destruction
and
lava flow to every landscape
of this life.

Cast fire and fury upon me.

Have Your way anywhere.

Incinerate all inhibition
and mediocrity.

Burn whatsoever You must,
and do so now!

Fortify the madness
of this conflagration.

Ignite a flaming passion
beyond describing.

Throw giant shadows
across the topography
of my forgetfulness.

Smolder within as intimation.

Immolate resistance
and half-heartedness
and
like the majesty of Kilauea*,
be unforgiving in Your destruction
of all that separates me from You.

Beloved Pele,
Goddess of Fire,
reduce me to ashes
and fling me at the feet
of
My Beloved,
forever!

*Kilauea on the Big Island of Hawai'i is one
of the most active volcanoes in the world.

Open wide these Tavern doors.

Pour wine.

Slip into your dancing shoes.

Come celebrate.

I am a married man now,
wedded to The One
who will never leave me.

My two-timing days are over.

I am responsible only
to The One I love.

It's signed, sealed, delivered.

Uncomfortable,
jealous,
even a little pissed perhaps?

I really don't care.

If you have a problem
with what I do,
that problem is yours.

Good luck putting me in a box.

I've had no success with that
endeavor,
however alluring
your gift-wrap might be.

You don't like the words I speak?

Leave.

Put me upon a pedestal?

You get to negotiate
the fallout of your projections.

It is not
that I don't love you anymore.

It is just that I am hooked on the
Wild One,
lock, stock and barrel.

Now The Beloved gazes upon you
through these eyes
with
a Love that knocks my socks off.

OPEN WIDE
THE DOORS

Through these ears
The Holy One
hears the humming of creation.

My Beloved
moves and speaks this body
and I am in wholehearted fidelity
to those impulses.

Behold a crazy mind
sinking in servitude
to a heart that is mine no longer.

I am out of the picture.

You think me insufferable,
undependable,
unpredictable,
insane?

I Am.

Hopefully some day
you will endure my company.

I need not
the benediction of your approval
nor the anointing of your validation.

Shower me with plumeria blossoms!

Pelt me with lava rock!

It happens all the time.

I will pick up neither.

This is a different dance now.

Hey,
why not join the celebration?

Step off your merry-go-round
and join this circus of insanity.

There is
more, more, more
than your wildest imaginings
awaiting us both.

Who knows,
you may bump into
The One who will never leave you?

And get married.

And then we will both be betrothed
to The One Vagabond
who wants us all!

Some call it bigamy.

I say *the more the merrier!*

ANOTHER
SLOPPY
LOVE
POEM

*D*on't expect
  another sloppy love poem
from me right now.

I am not in the mood
for sweet talk or tender words
today.

Come,
step into the shadows
if you have a constitution
for the dark side of Our Beloved
this evening.

Kick open the dungeon door
and enter the roughhouse
for a while.

I have been taken into slavery.

In servitude,
I have fallen heart over head,
into loving obedience,
to a Maniac!

My ankles are shackled.

My wrists are bound.

Anywhere other than here
with You,
my Master,
is hell.

The insanity of future and past
is more brutal than this surrender.

Beat me,
chain me
into the glory of The Immediate.

More, more, more
of You,
as me,
is my prayer without ceasing.

Harness the darkness,
bring on the light!

Pierce me
with Your Benevolence.

Brutalize me with Your Love.

Spank me out of a wanderlust
that never worked anyway.

I am Your slave.

Have Your way with me.

Strap me to Your rack
and
stretch me to places
I've not ventured before.

I will do anything for You.

This life is Yours now.

The renunciation,
absolute.

Handcuff me to Your heart
as
I lay my bloody and obedient life
at Your feet
in subservience,
forever and ever,
Amen.

THE GREAT STORY

*E*mbedded deep within you,
    from the very beginning,
is the Great Story of your life.

Fall to your knees.

Lay your ear to the ground.

Listen
for the melody of that Story.

Do you hear your Song?

It's there.

Rooted within you.

Always playing.

Beautiful beyond describing.

Awaiting your dancing.

Are you setting for anything
less than your Story,
your Song?

Return yourself to yourself.

Discover the Meaning
already seeded within you.

Embrace the Great Story
you have longed for,
for so long.

And as you die
to all the small stories
and little songs,
may the requiem of their passing
herald
the glory of your Homecoming.

Give way
into the sacred arc of your life.

Your Story.

Your Song.

Home.

HALLAJ

Hallaj* is my hero.

He died
to be the God he loved
and died again for that.

Now he has taken me
by the scruff of the neck
and hauled me through
the debris of my forgetfulness.

My Beloved,
am I as crazy
about You as Hallaj was?

I don't know,
but I am certainly willing to be.

My love for you
is a compulsive obsession.

I am willingly and thankfully
intoxicated
with You,
as You,
in You.

I will not prostitute this life
to mediocrity.

I am on fire at Your feet,
addicted,
and I need no twelve-step program.

Nail me to the stake.

Off with my head,
if that must be.

I am Your servant,
slave
and drunkard,
forever.

*Mansur al-Hallaj was born around 858 in Persia. He was a Sufi mystic, writer and teacher. While many felt it inappropriate to share mysticism with the masses, Al-Hallaj openly did so. He made enemies. His ecstatic states of adulation and exultation were controversial: I am The Truth! There is nothing under my cloak but God! These utterances led to a long trial and imprisonment in Baghdad before he was publicly beheaded in 922.

*Cry out! Don't be stolid and silent
with your pain. Lament! And let the milk
of loving flow into you.*

—*Rumi*

FIRE

I was five years old when the moonlight stopped seducing me. The curtains turned bright every month and my bedroom door remained closed. I did not see the midnight snowdrops again, nor did I adore the magnolia blossoms in a light that once protected me.

I no longer felt safe at home. I was terrified of my father's mercurial behavior. The arguments were unnerving. The darkness scared me. When I was ten years old, boarding school severed the cord to my magic life completely. The surreptitious and unwelcomed bodies in my bed destroyed the safety of night. Boys and teachers, who had their way with me in darkness, tormented and bullied me in the light of day.

After graduating from high school in 1967, a year of conscripted military service opened a window into the hatred and violence underlying my privileged white life. Weapons of war, tear gas and the truncheons of apartheid eventually catapulted me way beyond my bloodstained country to a bigger and bewildering world far away. Wandering to distant lands, a darkness deeper than a moonless night entered my bloodstream, shattering the hopes and dreams of a lifetime.

———— ❧ ————

After my first retreat with Joseph Goldstein, I lived for a year at the Buddhist Retreat Centre before returning in 1982 to the world I had left behind in New York City. I was shaken to discover that my old life seemed meaningless. The Persian rugs, treasures and paintings from around the world felt burdensome. The view of the Hudson River, Statue of Liberty and the Empire State Building through my apartment windows meant nothing anymore. There was no enthusiasm for my career. I was no longer enthralled by the gay lifestyle I once enjoyed. The call of silence and a much simpler life was undeniable. After much agonizing, I eventually gave all I possessed to my younger brother Craig, who had immigrated to Canada. I

shaved my head and entered a monastery.

The early 1980s was a terrifying time in the gay community. We knew that something devastating was happening. Friends were unaccountably sick, emaciated and dying. No one knew why.

I had one final and fateful fling before entering the holy life. I saw him the moment I entered the bar. He stood in the semi-darkness holding a beer, leaning against the wall. A cap hung down over his forehead. He was slim and handsome. He stared at me. I walked over. Despite my feelings of caution, I reluctantly accompanied him home. In his bedroom were photographs of a strapping and muscular man I almost did not recognize. I wanted to flee and could not. Paralyzed with fear, I sublimated my will to a stranger.

After several months at the monastery I fell seriously ill, not knowing that the HIV virus was establishing itself in my body. Ten years later, as I grappled with the legacy of sexual abuse, I finally understood why my courage had failed me that fateful night, why I could not say *No* and why I so often felt a victim of circumstance.

———— ❧ ————

I returned to South Africa in 1989 to be with two friends who were living with AIDS. Roy died as my plane landed and Michael not long thereafter.

I stayed with my parents for a few weeks. One evening my father left for bed, complaining of a pain in his stomach and chest. Adelaide and I settled into an evening of cards in the living room. His snoring accompanied us as we sipped rooibos tea, chatted and enjoyed our game. Suddenly a ghastly sound broke the reverie. We rushed to the bedroom. My father was sitting up in bed. His body

shook wildly as he flailed and beat his chest. I called the doctor. Adelaide and I moved to either side of his bed, holding him and whispering words of encouragement. His pain was enormous. A huge spasm shook his body, his back arched and he slumped onto the pillow, limp and lifeless in our arms.

Two months later, back in the United States, I sat in a doctor's office, sick and exhausted.

I knew that the information of the next minutes would change my life forever. I either had sidestepped AIDS or would begin a journey traveled by many of my friends. The doctor walked in. Words were unnecessary. The expression upon his face was more informative than any diagnosis could ever be. The first words that crossed my mind were *I will not be defined by this virus. I am greater than the journey I'm about to begin.* And then my life hit the fan.

After taking care of medical matters, I returned once again to the Insight Meditation Society for a long retreat with Joseph Goldstein. Sitting way back in the meditation hall, I was overwhelmed by the magnitude of emotions pouring through me. In meditation I engaged the feelings, even when it felt almost impossible to do so.

Facing myself honestly was hell. I had to admit that I was not the angel I once perceived myself to be. To be free from suffering I sensed the importance of finding a way to allow the fear, anger and disappointment to move without argument within me, the same emotions I had largely denied and suppressed for all my life. Their emergence on retreat was terrifying and humbling. I was roasting on my meditation cushion, haunted by memories.

One day in the meditation hall I fell backwards, off my cushion, alarming everyone nearby. Joseph suggested I meditate in my room for a while. A sickening stench of tobacco smoke filled my little room. The staff investigated and assured me that no one was smoking in the vicinity. I kept at it. During my meditations, I gradually discerned the imprint and pressure of a hand on my face before I was pushed again. Not long afterwards, as I again tumbled backwards to the floor, I recognized a familiar face. His tobacco-stained hand covered my nose and mouth while he fondled my genitals. I was an infant. The images and physical sensations were clearer than the little marble Buddha sitting on my altar. The rage was volcanic. Grief, terror and sadness were with me day and night.

Joseph explained that one of the meditations offered by the Buddha for practicing mindfulness of the body is to open to the elements of which it is comprised: earth, water, fire and air. I opened to the emotional energies as expressions of those elements. I felt the hot, cold or neutral sensations of the fire element, the hard or soft sensations of the earth element and the stagnant or moving sensations of water within my body. When mindful of the sensations of the breath in meditation, I was in relationship with the air element. This practice helped me move below the proliferation of thoughts and stories to a more visceral experience of the emotional energies moving through me.

I soon realized that my endeavors to avoid the pain were even more excruciating than accepting what was occurring. Gradually I was able to simply feel the emotions without turning them into a drama in my mind.

In 2004 I lived for a year on the east side of Hawai'i near Kilauea, the active volcano on the Big Island. Out of my bedroom window the sky was blood red at night. Clouds and fog were illuminated by a huge lake of lava within one of the craters towards the top of the mountain. I made frequent pilgrimages to the volcano. One evening, in the moonlight, I came upon a white owl standing on the black lava before me. She gazed piercingly into my eyes. Neither of us moved. I placed a bunch of white lilies before the bird, my offering for the Goddess Pele.

Underfoot, the lava got warmer and warmer as I continued my hike. The smell of melting rubber from my boots accelerated my pace as I scrambled over mounds of crispy, sharp and jagged stone. After many hours, I reached a molten landscape at the water's edge. Blood-red waves crashed against the fiery flow as it entered the ocean.

The Buddhist Elements collided in dynamic majesty all around me. Shards of fine glass ricocheted through clouds of sulfuric acid as balls of fire crisscrossed the sky. I felt like a hobbit before the glory of Mount Doom. I rested for a moment upon a pile of lava rock, silenced by the magnificence surrounding me. As I stepped away the ground opened like a flower, pouring lava at my feet. Within minutes I was standing within a field of fire.

It is a dangerous madness to be on the ocean's edge with active lava. It is not unusual for huge banks of unstable coastline to dislodge and fall into the water. I dodged and leapt, carrying my trembling heart back to safety.

SHORTCUT TO HEAVEN

There is no shortcut to Heaven.

You will not leap
to The Kingdom
without stumbling.

This is a long enduring road,
where every part of you
shall be rendered holy and lovely
by your willingness
to falter and fall
upon your Great Adventure.

Fasten your seatbelt.

Expect turbulence.

It's part of the curriculum.

Never give up!

For within
the sacredness of failure,
staggering to the left,
veering to the right,
flat upon your face,
awash with tears,
you will come to know
what Heaven is not.

Neti, neti*,
neither this, nor that.

Are your footfalls
redolent with frustration
and
the disintegration
of your dreaming?

No idea where you're going?

Don't stop!

Remember,
you have turned
towards The Unknowable,
where you will discover
a Heaven upon earth
infinitely more beautiful
than you ever imagined.

Your notions of Love?

One tiny star
within galaxies of illumination.

Your thoughts of Freedom?

A single petal
opening
within fields in bloom.

Your imaginings of Joy?

One drop
within an ocean of happiness,
awaiting your arrival.

Every preconception will fail.

Neti, neti,
neither this, nor that.

A quest for security
along the way?

I don't think so.

Travel insurance?

Unavailable.

No Google map.

No yellow brick road.

Neti, neti,
neither this, nor that.

Arise from
the sacred ground of failure!

Begin again,
again and again.

Trailing blood.

Checkmated.

Weeping and wailing
if that must be.

Neti, neti,
neither this, nor that.

And the day shall dawn
when you will give thanks
for all the setbacks.

They were trumpets
heralding your Homecoming.

There were no mistakes,
wrong turns
or stumbling blocks.

Every failure,
a portal to the perfection
of who you Truly are.

Frozen
before the headlights
of The Divine,
you will laugh without ceasing.

You were within
The Gates of Heaven
from the very beginning!

Neti, neti,
neither this, nor that,
all the way Home.

* *"Neti, Neti" is a Sanskrit phrase found in the
Upanishads—a sacred Hindu text—meaning
"neither this, nor that," pointing towards
The Wordless and Infinite.*

CARNIVAL

*I*s your life a frantic dash
   from what has been
to the to-do list
of what may yet be in store for you?

Spinning in circles?

Dizzy?

Disconnected?

Have you joined
the carnival of insanity
sweeping the land?

Time available, never enough?

Are you moving at the speed of light?

And is this the light you long for?

There is nothing courageous
or valiant about such frenzy.

Rushing from fire to fire is no fun,
and not without consequence.

Stop before you are stopped
by the reverberations
of speeding and acceleration.

Move more slowly,
without apology or justification.

You may wish to also disdain the
exhausting spiritual merry-go-round
of cultivation,
self-improvement and purification.

Stop seeking!

You are already all that you yearn for,
and so much more.

Decry the voices of poverty and lack.

If there's a problem
it's one of momentum, not deficit.

Freefall from small-time
into the depths of time.

Rest within The Web
from which you cannot fall, ever.

Encounter all who have been,
are,
and will be,
within The Timeless Immediate.

Future and past are present here.

Nothing to flee, nowhere to go.

Fall to your knees.

Drink the sacrament of Deep Time.

Recognize yourself within
The Great Interconnectedness
as every jewel,
everything,
everyone,
everywhere.

Be dazzled by the realm of reflection
and refraction.

Move from stillness, like The Tao.

Upon The Great Way
you will find balance,
harmony,
rest
and infinite evolution,
without rushing.

Live with deep eyes.

The Tao is not hurtling
towards its own conclusions or agenda.

Neither need you.

Stop as the Buddha did,
under the Bodhi Tree.

Set the sails of your weary heart
to the eye of the storm
where the weather is calm.

Sense The Still Ground
of Limitless Silence
that is always there,
into which all weather conditions
come and go.

Be The Stillness,
which you are.

Move as Love moves,
dancing all the way Home,
for Home
is the only real happiness
and
true rest there is.

SLEEPWALKING WITHIN A DREAM

What if you could no longer see
the sky and the sun,
the rain or the rainbows?

What if the moon,
the stars
and the shadows of night
were lost to you,
forever?

No doubt a great sadness
would befall your beautiful heart.

For until the Eyes within your eyes
can see again,
the great owls of night
are gone,
as
are the dragonflies and butterflies
of your days.

See the world once again like a child.

Innocent.

Naked.

Honest.

Simple.

Unscripted by thought.

For when a label,
which is a thought,
is placed upon anything,
there is overshadowing and loss.

All we see is the thought.

We perceive
through a filter of our thinking.

The original thing,
lost to us,
perhaps for ever.

Trance-walkers,
sleepwalking
within a dream of our creation.

The clouds,
breezes and birds,
disappeared!

Heartbreaking, isn't it?

Until we are willing to travel deeper
than fixation upon thought,
we miss
the simple, naked glory of creation,
as it is,
as it is,
as it is right now!

Are you willing to abandon
your love affair
with the language of your mind,
and get Real?

Are you satisfied
slumbering through life,
in love with your thinking?

And is that the love affair
you really want?

The choice is yours.

No matter how glorious,
burnished,
spiritual,
or eloquent,
thoughts are always
a deflection from The Truth.

But please, don't believe me.

You may not want to believe
what you're thinking right now,
either.

Find out for yourself.

Stop.

Look.

Witness.

Observe.

Inquire.

All those thoughts of you?

No more who you are
than the passing of clouds,
the waving of grasses
or the falling of nuts.

Your views and opinions
about the Milky Way?

Not the Milky Way.

There is no Milky Way!

Crazy, isn't it?

We are inmates
within an insane asylum.

Thinking is not the problem.

Allow thoughts to come and go.

Don't root within them.

Don't believe them either.

They're not who you are.

Move deeper!

Rest in that of you
which is larger
than any thought could ever be.

Hark!

The orchestra is playing your Song.

The dance floor awaits you.

Don't hesitate.

Don't think about it!

Just dance, dance, dance,
all the way Home!

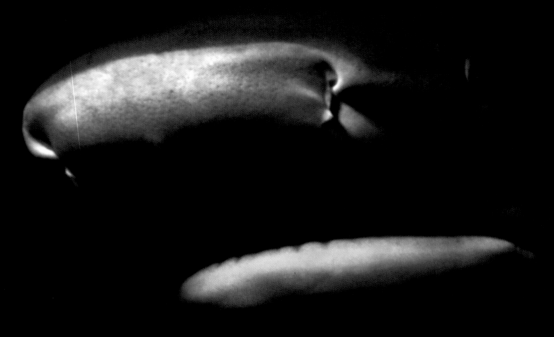

RESIST
NOT

*R*esist not the difficult person
  standing before you right now.

This one is a Divine Emissary
pointing towards that within you,
ready to join
The Great Story of your life.

Feel your connection with this one.

It is there, like it or not.

Be not against
what is given you.

Whatever is rejected
obscures the glory
of who you truly are.

Give
what you want the most from others.

Hear the Hounds of Heaven
yapping at your ankles.

The Assembly of Angels
is already singing
your song of Homecoming.

Don't procrastinate a moment longer.

Stop the war.

Welcome
the wild winds of circumstance
and the challenges before you,
Emissaries all,
from Our Beloved,
calling you Home
without delay.

Disdain
the subterfuge
of separation and resistance,
however eloquent
the dexterity of your justification
might be.

Keep your eyes on The Prize
of
this precious, precious life.

Fortify what you are for,
not against.

For
Our Beloved
will continue to provide you
with Emissaries
until it is no longer necessary
to do so.

SPIRITUAL RESUME

Leave your spiritual resume
   outside the door,
no matter how illustrious or eloquent
it may be.

I am not interested
in your itinerary either,
however holy, exalted and rarefied your
destinations may have been.

The illuminated travelers
you have come upon along the way?

Don't bother.

Please,
shelve your lineage
of books, CDs and retreats
you have aced.

Rather,
tell me what lives
within the slipstream
of your high adventuring,
right now!

What of The Holy Places
within yourself,
to which you have journeyed?

Let me know the Wisdom and Love
of your great teachers,
percolating within you at this time.

What are the lessons you've learned
with humility and through fire?

Sadness?

Caring?

Rage?

Tenderness?

Terror?

Has your love of Truth
superseded your need
for comfort and distraction?

Are you a lover of True Love now,
or not?

How is The Dazzling Darkness
these days?

Tell me of
Silence and The Unknowable,
here,
now.

Have all the vortexes
and sacred places you have known
devolved into a freedom
that lives within you now?

Or not?

You see,
sacredness by association,
osmosis
and tabulation
is just more
accumulation,
and a visit to the mall will provide
similar fleeting pleasures,
at a fraction of the cost!

THE SPARKS OF YOUR HEART

*D*o you thirst for a lightening rod
towards which the angry sparks
of your heart can fly?

Is there a frantic search
for an object of disaffection
every time
your happiness is interrupted?

Is there a need for enemies out there
as circumstances shift
from favorable to unfavorable?

Are you blaming yourself?

Someone else?

Or is it a thing you're blaming?

The weather conditions perhaps?

A shift in the ether?

A configuration of the planets?

Aliens?

A life of blaming never
ceases,
ever!

Dispatching a search party
to identify the enemy
is a road to nowhere.

And when your center of gravity
is out there, where are you?

Anger is not the problem.

Rage is not the problem.

Fury is not the problem.

Any unwillingness
to feel the energy of rage,
anger,
fury moving within you
is the problem.

Bow before the footfalls
of the immediate.

Be humbled at the altar
of self-acknowledgment.

Be human!

Here lies
the landscape of Peace and Love
you long for.

Believing the fiction of
right and wrong,
bad and good,
friends and enemies,
hardens a heart already broken
by the sorrow of separation
and the agony of blame.

And yet,
nestling
within the palm of your hand

right now,
is the key to ending
your thirst for enemies, for all time.

Stop.

Recognize.

Accept.

Feel.

Allow.

Befriend

Everything.

Now.

Including anger, rage, fury!

Turn the key.

Push open the door,
from the inside!

You never left Home, ever!

It was all a dream

LOST
IN TRANSLATION

40

*A*re you living a lateral life,
looking for Home
where it cannot be?

Plying the horizontal
for significance and meaning
as you skim the surface
of your sacred life?

Populating
the smorgasbord out there,
gathering experience
upon experience
unto yourself?

Dipping,
sipping,
accumulating.

Where more is better
and less will just not do.

A junkie,
looking for the next spiritual fix,
while frustrating
the depths of who you really are.

Seeking this?

Searching for that?

Paradise lost?

Paradise found?

Stop!

Sparks will surely fly.

Lights will flash.

Your hackles will rise and fall.

Energy will exit
every orifice of your body,
or not.

Visions will arise,
terrible and titillating,
both.

Psychic windows
will open and close.

Apparitions will arise
and pass away.

Your teeth will chatter.

Your knees will knock.

Your heart will overflow
with love and fear.

And you will stumble.

You will burp.

You will fumble.

You will fart!

Don't get lost
within your translation of experiences,
giving them a significance
they do not have.

You may not wish to gauge
your spiritual evolution
within this neighborhood either.

All experiences come and go,
that is their nature.

At best,
road stops
upon your journey Home,
by-products of waking up,
not Awakening itself.

Turn towards Ground Zero now,
The Oneness out of which
all experiences are born
and to which they return.

Devolve into Sacred Ground
where disappearance is impossible.

Plummet to the
depths of who you are.

Surrender into the vertical.

Follow the deep thread of your precious,
blessed life,
and you shall come upon
your True Nature,
not by design nor will,
but by happenstance and Grace.

And all your experiences
will be welcomed,
lived,
and known for what they are
and
for what they never could be.

Now you are freed
from vicissitudes forever,
standing upon
The Unchanging Ground of Nowhere.

HOSTILE TAKEOVER

I am checking in,
   My Beloved.

We are in agreement
that between us
there will be no secrets,
ever?

Good!

Well, here's the thing.

At the moment I am bewildered,
unhappy
and
rather pissed off with You.

This Homecoming
feels more like a hostile takeover
than a benevolence these days.

Humbling.

Relentless.

An annihilation.

A humiliation.

Are You a nasty response
to desperate prayer?

A Holy Slap in the face,
when I'm down
upon my bloody knees?

In Deuteronomy I have read
that You are a jealous,
angry
and unforgiving God.

It certainly feels that way right now.

However,
let me not be hasty.

I'll take a breath.

Calm down.

Reaction will get me nowhere.

Oh my God!

I'm getting a taste of what
The Good Book
has been saying all along.

Finally!

You are unforgiving
of all that fragments me.

Angry with all that obscures
Your open doorway.

Jealous of all that separates me
from You!

Wow!

I have to be careful what I pray for.

You are no small potatoes!

DIVINE
NARCISSIST

44

You are The Divine Narcissist,
    My Beloved.

It's all about You,
isn't it?

You will neither rest
nor give me peace
until
all of me abides as all of You,
for You,
within You,
for all time.

There is no
margin for my narcissism
anymore.

Wow!

There You go again,
undermining the superstructure of
my inflation.

Flaunting
Your preeminence.

Taunting
me with One-upsmanship.

Tantalizing me
with intimations
of Your Unsurpassing Glory.

You are a shameless One.

This is narcissism wars,
and my narcissism
is no match for Yours!

I give up!

I'm out of here!

Me?

All Yours now!

ONE FELL SWOOP

*M*y Beloved,
    You reach relentlessly
into my humanity,
dragging forth all that is untouched
by the glory of Your Love,
beautifying
every part of me.

Coming back for Yourself,
as me,
wherever Your Majesty
is obscured.

I do have one request though?

Let's get this over with,
already!

I am awed
by this re-collection of Yourself.

Amazed
with the perfection of the integration.

Humbled
by the self-acknowledgment
You demand of this weathered heart.

What more do you want?

I am being slapped around
so much
I don't even miss You
when You use the restroom!

How weird is that?

Maybe I am losing my mind as well!

How about
one,
big,
wild,
divine,
fell swoop?

Bang!

And then all of me
will be boogieboarding
with all of You,
forever and ever,
Amen.

Stay together, friends.
Don't scatter and sleep.
Our friendship is made
of being awake.

—*Rumi*

TOGETHERNESS

Invisibility and hiding were the tools of my early survival. Those impulses accompanied me into adulthood, complicating my life and affecting those around me. Coming into true relationship with others has not been a simple endeavor.

Emerging from isolation is an ongoing journey. Discovering connectedness and communion has been a long and winding road. Step-by-step, circumstance-by-circumstance, my willing footfalls have inclined towards deepening intimacy with those around me.

After my HIV diagnosis in the summer of 1989, a circle of friends and neighbors in Massachusetts formed a support group for me. We met once a month as I negotiated the challenges of those years. I faced my incapacity to ask for assistance and my reluctance to accept their support and kindness. If I was going to survive I had to relinquish my wish to do everything myself. They taught me how to ask for help and graciously accept it.

Their love surrounded me on a retreat that fall. I felt fragile and alone, surrounded by the fragments of a life that once promised much. I prayed for one more year of life and the opportunity to tie up loose ends. The imminence of death nudged me from every direction. The assumption of "a tomorrow" died. One evening Joseph Goldstein quoted the words of the Buddha: *Friendship, companionship and association with good and noble people is the whole of the holy life.* The

blessing of being in community with others on that retreat was immeasurable.

In December 1998 I flew to Hawai'i to escape the harsh Massachusetts winter. When the wheels of the plane hit the runway in Hilo on the Big Island, my heart whispered, *You're home, kid!* My mind said, *You're crazy! You have a home, support group and friends on the East Coast. Here, you know no one.* I loved being in the tropics. The flowers, ocean and balmy weather were reminiscent of my Africa. Within a week it was unthinkable that I be anywhere else. I sold my home and settled into a new life. The love of my New England community unfurled my wings wide enough to begin a new adventure. Able to reach out more easily, a new community came together around the spiritual teachings I have offered in Hawai'i.

In 2006 the pull of Africa was strong. I had not been back for six years. My doctor's advice was sobering. *You must understand that a return to Africa might kill you. Untreatable tuberculosis and viral meningitis are endemic to the area you will be visiting.* Before I left, the community organized a big farewell party.

I returned again to the Buddhist Retreat Centre in South Africa. The Ofafa Valley has one of the highest incidences of AIDS in the world. I was nervous as I walked towards the buildings of the Woza Moya Project, a grassroots community organization that serves all who are affected by AIDS in the area, including orphaned and vulnerable children (See Appendix 3).

A young boy ran up to me with open arms. His T-shirt read, "Whatever." Bodily fluids wept from every orifice of his body. His nose, eyes, ears and penis were red and inflamed. I was face to face with AIDS in Africa! Terror

and hesitation froze my heart for a moment before reaching down and opening my arms to the child. I crossed the line and took my place within a community of brothers and sisters in Africa, each of us together finding our way with a common virus. It was a relief. My friends at the Woza Moya Project are family now. The poem "Children of Africa" is a tribute to the young ones I met.

Another party awaited me upon my return to Hawai'i. Now I was a blessed with two communities, on opposite sides of the planet! I assembled a slideshow and wept while sharing stories of Africa, particularly those of the Woza Moya Project. My Hawai'i community responded with an outpouring of love and generosity. Funds flowed in and eventually $130,000 was raised to pay for schooling, books and uniforms for innumerable children. We funded a water well, fed families in need, and in partnership with others built a huge Children's Center which has given thousands of young ones a center of gravity within the instability and insecurity of their lives.

⸻ ⟡ ⸻

In Hawai'i I lived for six years in a home on the beach. Every morning I swam out to the reef. The ocean was my refuge. The fish, whales, dolphins, turtles, sharks, manta rays and octopi were my family! The beauty of the Hawaiian Green Sea Turtle captivated me. One day I came upon an emaciated turtle lying on the sand in shallow waters. A fishing float was wedged outside its mouth.

Every evening dozens of turtles gathered in a pond right in front of my home, their sanctuary from the sharks at night. The injured turtle arrived also. I contacted the Hawai'i State Sea Turtle Rescue Team and together we dislodged a huge fishing hook deeply embedded within its throat. Using a drill and white, waterproof paint, we marked the carapace before releasing her back into the water. At dusk each day she returned to the pond and then one day stopped coming.

A few years later, with the support of my neighbors, I arranged a community gathering at a local church to draw attention to the endangered turtles and how to better protect them. Hawaiian elders talked about the legends of the turtles. On the day of the event, I was joined by a turtle who swam below me and would not leave. When I turned left, she turned left. I turned right, so did she. I examined her well-worn carapace. There, weathered and almost indistinct, were the markings we had made years before. She was beautiful and in great shape!

⸻ ⟡ ⸻

Brandvlei Prison is a maximum-security facility near Worcester in the Western Cape of South Africa. While it may be the end of the line for many hardcore criminals, it is also the birthplace of an extraordinary miracle. In 2011, I spent several days with a number of men incarcerated for murder, battery, use of weapons and theft. In the most challenging of circumstances, they have grappled with the forces of violence and rage within themselves, faced their crimes and discovered a field of Love that touches everyone they meet, inside the barbed wire and beyond. They call themselves the Group of Hope and are resolved to do whatever possible to demonstrate remorse and make a difference in the world (See Appendix 4).

Just before saying goodbye to my new friends, I read the poem "Missing the Mark," a tribute to seven of the most beautiful hearts I have known. I was nervous and self-conscious. When I looked up, we were all in tears. When the warden eventually escorted me outside, the men handed me a big, folded piece of blue cardboard. Inside were seven hearts and within each heart was a love letter of thanks, gratitude and brotherhood.

The words of Desmond Tutu accompanied me home:

One of the sayings in South Africa is Ubuntu, the essence of being human. We cannot exist as human beings in isolation. It speaks about our interconnectedness. We can't be human all by ourselves, and when we have this quality, Ubuntu, we are known for our generosity. We think of ourselves far too frequently as just individuals, separated from one another, whereas we are connected and what we do affects the whole world. When we do well it spreads out; it is for the whole of humanity.

WE
WALK
TOGETHER

We walk hand in hand
wherever you are,
wherever I find myself.

We walk body to body
no matter where
the footsteps of our lives take us.

We walk heart to heart
in whatever direction
the unfolding of Love moves us.

We walk and play together
within every corridor
of this precious and blessed life,
even when our footfalls
appear to move differently.

We walk mind to mind,
The One Mind
resting within The Unknowable.

We walk eye to eye,
perceiving the arising of The One
coming into form
and returning
to The Infinite Mystery that we are,
as we walk together.

EVIDENCE WITHOUT PROSECUTION

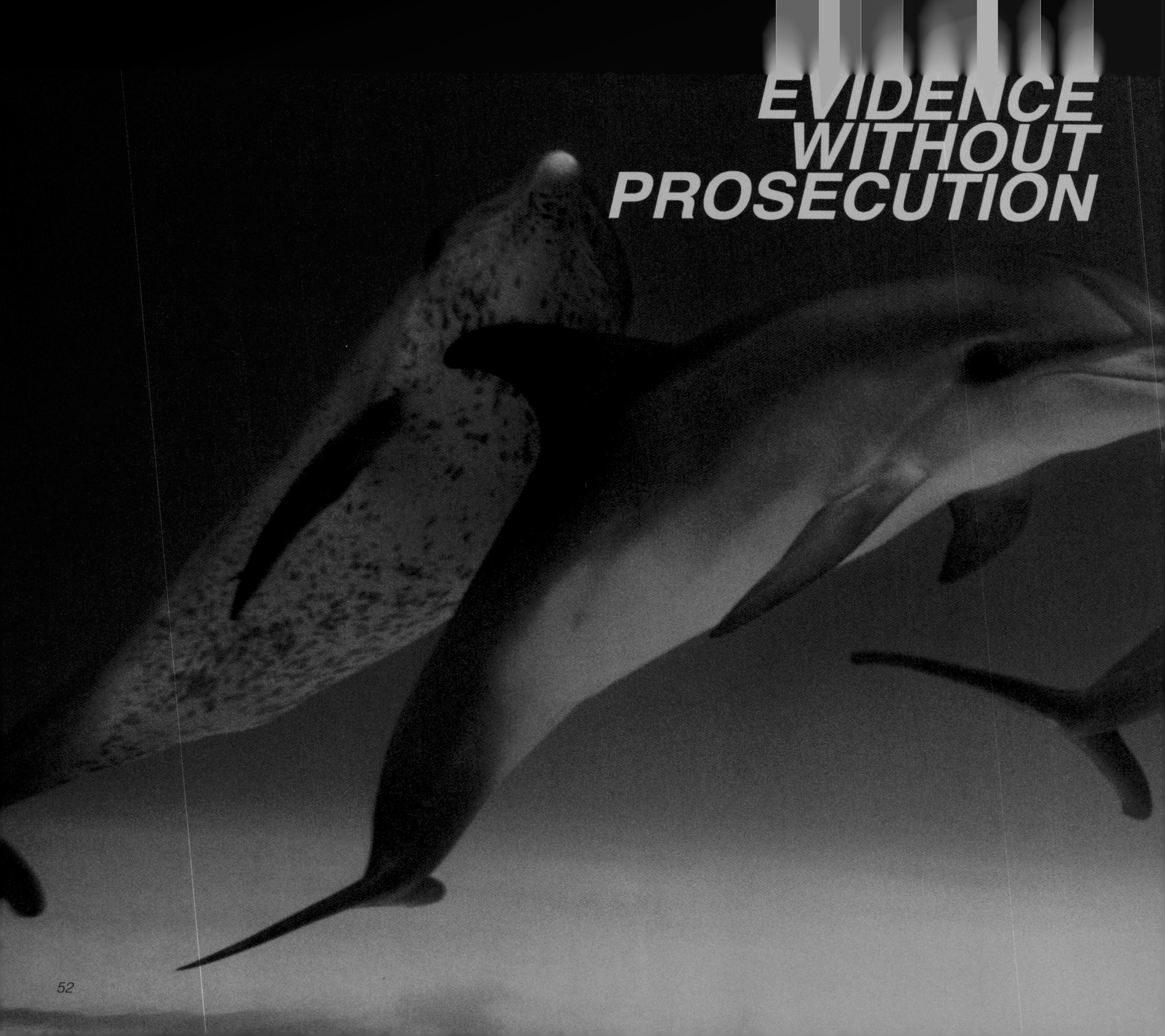

*P*lease take my hand
     and walk beside me
as
we cross the threshold
of this quivering heart together.

This is not a pretty picture.

Keep moving.

We are not here
to re-enter a life
that is dead and gone forever.

Witness around you
the scar tissue
of sixty years of forgetfulness,
all evidence without prosecution.

Hear the silence of the deep.

Sense the fragrance of Holy Ground.

Nervous?

I am.

Stand close.

This is the place where I turned away
from My Beloved,
long, long ago.

This is the *NO*
that sourced the train wreck
we have evidenced
upon our journey
to this sacred landscape.

Please kneel beside me
as
I bow before the altar of this lifetime
and turn back
towards The One I left behind.

That *NO* is no longer.

The jig is up!

Do you feel my thankfulness
ricocheting around this sacred moment,
as
Love illuminates this Tavern to its rafters?

May the joy here join your own,
in celebration
of the One Joy we all are,
as we dance together
forever and ever,
Amen.

THE
DAMN
CLOSET
DOOR

Come over my friend.

Let us lean
against this closet door
together.

Enter my story,
I will join yours,
and
perhaps the weight
of all that has been
will budge
these bloody hinges
once and for all.

I want out.

You want out.

We are in this together.

Let's not wait
a moment longer,
for the drama of me
and
that of you
gets heavier all the time.

This air is fetid with
forgetfulness
and
the trance of sleepwalking.

Hear
the howling discontent,
our joined disaffection
with these
carefully choreographed
lives of contraction
and control.

Allow our longing
to lean into this door
with the gravity
of interwoven resolve,
our hearts hell-bent
on breaking free together.

We've been inside
this damn closet
far too long!

Push.

Heave.

Oh my goodness.

Did you feel
the door open just a little?

Quick, take my hand.

Let's fall to our knees
across this sacred threshold,
while the portal is ajar
and before
the door closes again.

Shut your eyes.

Bow your head.

The light of Our Beloved
can be blinding
within such darkness.

Step out of a hell
that has imprisoned us
longer than memory,
and
witness the disintegration
of our dreaming.

Amazing, isn't it?

Look.

The story of me is toast.

You too.

My God,
we are stark naked
before Our Beloved,
who is grinning with relief
at us,
as us,
with us,
in welcome and celebration.

Done
is what had to be done
my friend!

We are The Silence
within
which the music plays!

How cool is that?

The Stillness
within which
all movement dances!

Knocks one's socks off,
doesn't it?

The Nothingness
within which
The Glory of Creation
has its way.

It doesn't get any better
than this!

Whatever else can we do
stark naked,
but dance together,
forever and ever,
Amen.

THE CHILDREN OF AFRICA

This poem is dedicated to the orphaned and vulnerable children of Africa.

*T*hrow yourself to the ground
    before the children of Africa.

Allow your heart to harmonize
with the drumbeat
of the Great Continent.

Taste the soil as sacrament
and ancient memory.

For this is the landscape
from which we all came,
and to which you now return.

These young ones
stand upon the ground
of your deepest belonging.

    Be blinded
        by the radiance of young eyes
            witnessing your homecoming,
                for those who have nothing
                    may have everything
                        for you today.

Gaze into the glory
of a child
without accumulation.

Be naked before those unclothed
within
privilege and entitlement.

Pray before the tears of ones
neglected into violence and poverty.

These children are unschooled
in hope, promise and security.

And bowing before those
who have little,
may we find a thankfulness
for all we have been given.

And within the morning mist
rising across the Ofafa Valley
and touching the walls
of Woza Moya* today,
let us kneel before the mirror
before us.

And may the lifting of clouds within
reveal the innocence we are,
were
and
always will be.

And may
God Bless Africa
and Her children,
forever.

Nkosi Sikelel' iAfrika.**

*See the Woza Moya Project,
Appendix 3.

**Nkosi Sikelel' iAfrika *is the
National Liberation Anthem of South Africa,
translated as* God Bless Africa.

ME
AND THE
MAC NUTS

I live in community now,
  a cast of millions.

Me and the macadamia nuts,
at play
in The Fields of The Infinite.

An orchard of mischief.

A landscape of high adventuring.

I once lived exclusively under
the Gavin tree.

Alone,
separate,
fragmented,
isolated,
seemingly forgotten by everyone,
even God.

Apparently overlooked,
but not!

For under
the blue full New Year's moon
I recognized You, My Beloved,

as every macnut,
blade of grass,
crab spider,
moonbeam
and
shadow in the community.

Wild Trickster that You are.

And oh!
how we danced.

Clumsy steps.

Slipping on the fallen nuts,
giggling,
silly,
singing,
frightening the pigs,
terrifying the turkeys,
falling in the mud,
intoxicated,
reveling within one another.

And glancing back across time
to the Gavin Tree,
I saw You,

My Beloved,
scratching your head
in bewilderment,
puzzled,
wondering:

*How the hell
could you ever have wished
to hide under that solitary tree,
Gavin,
when all of Creation has been
begging you to come out
and play all along?*

MISSING
THE MARK

This poem is dedicated to the men of the Group of Hope*:
Luyanda, Skoji, Pieter, Rasta, Orrie, Maaga and Sihle.

60

*Is there no end to Your surprises,
    My Beloved?*

*Just yesterday
I was flat upon my face again
before seven of Your Holy Ones,
archers all,
who certainly missed their mark**
big time.*

*Unspoken words
hovered around my trembling heart
as we gathered
  in the prison courtyard.*

Murder.

Robbery.

Weapons.

Assault.

*Life sentence,
    upon life sentence.*

        *And then
    You moved swiftly,
      releasing
      an accurate arrow
      from Your sacred bow,
      fully opening my eyes
    to the seven fires of love
    standing before me.*

    *More blinding
    than the African sun above.*

      Dazzling beyond describing.

And I saw, My Beloved, I saw!

*Their actions were terrible,
inexcusable.*

They missed their mark.

*Yet they were never bad,
evil,
sinners, ever!*

Their aim was faulty.

*And all I could see
were seven beautiful Buddhas
standing before me,
decked out in orange
like monks from Thailand.*

Hearts as wide as the world.

*"CORRECTIONS" emblazoned
across their overalls,
challenging me and the world,*

Wake up!

Stop missing the mark!

Look what happened to us!

This is my prayer:

*My Beloved,
may these brothers
remember without forgetting,
ever again,
who they really are.*

*Wildly fortify their loving
as they negotiate
the reverberations of consequence.*

*Allow their luminosity
to move out into the world
in every direction.*

*How could any incarceration
contain the majesty
of such true and irrepressible hearts?*

*And may all of us,
whichever side of the barbed wire
or prison bars we dwell,
come home to who we really are,
right now.*

Bless us with the finest of archery skills.

*For we are all prisoners
of our forgetfulness,
missing the mark,
until we hit The Divine Target
once again,
the limitless Love
that we always were,
are
and forever will be.*

*As the seven Holy Ones
in Brandvlei Prison
so eloquently reminded me,
yesterday.*

*See the Group of Hope, Appendix 4.

***Within the ancient Aramaic language of
Christ, the root word* satah—*an archery term
meaning that which causes us to miss the
mark—has traditionally been translated as* sin,
with all the associated connotations.

Dance, when you're broken open.
Dance, if you've torn the bandage off.
Dance in the middle of fighting.
Dance in your blood.
Dance, when you're perfectly free.

—Rumi

THE INDESCRIBABLE

It is not unusual to find oneself drenched to the bone while walking in the early morning mists of Waipio Valley in Hawai'i or the Ofafa Valley in Africa. For me the adventure of Awakening has been mostly like that—a gradual soaking, with intermittent bolts of clarity, just like lightning piercing the depths of an African thunderstorm.

Awakening is a death in life, and a returning. Gone is the illusion of who and what I previously thought myself to be. The significance of the dream world I cherished has evaporated. Today I know that I am limitlessly larger than the smallness I once lived. At last I have returned to the innocence of my magical garden, seasoned and aged by the passage of time.

Death and life feel deeply interwoven. Upon death's doorstep, The Deathless has twice met me and returned me back to human life.

I was admitted to hospital in Northampton Massachusetts, a few weeks after the publication of *In the Lap of the Buddha* in 1994. My temperature was 106.7°. Doctors anticipated irreparable brain damage or death. I had lost thirty pounds.

I was drenched in sweat, drugged and dull. One night I was jolted awake, my mind clear and alert. Surrounding me in every direction was a deep and comforting velvet blackness. Below me, stretching to a pinpoint in the distance, a river of salmon-colored rose petals. They shimmered and glowed in contrast to the pitch-black environment. Sitting cross-legged, a fraction above the river, I effortlessly skimmed the surface. Where the river disappeared, far in the distance, a bright white light shone back towards me. Bathed, saturated and infused with light and love, I felt safe and protected as the light reached out and I moved towards it. My heart exploded with joy and recognition. The forgotten and familiar Love was back! The closer I got, the stronger the Love.

Then my mind got busy. *This is amazing. I am dying. It's beautiful. The book is published. I have remembered the trustworthy Love of my magical garden.* A glimmer of self-satisfaction joined the proceedings. Instantly I made a ninety-degree turn and fell straight into the blackness to my right. My eyes opened. I was back in the hospital, surrounded by nurses and life-support equipment. The fever broke. The crisis was over.

The abiding memory is of the loving light and an unshakable sense that death is a return to Boundless Love, a short step from one garden to another.

In 2004 lights flashed and sirens wailed as an ambulance rushed across the runway in Waimea, Hawai'i to a tiny plane where medical personnel flew me to a hospital in Honolulu. I was admitted into an intensive care unit. *There are two options and one decision you have to make,* the surgeon told

me. *I must enter your lungs, perform a biopsy and withdraw fluid to make a diagnosis. There is no time for a general anesthetic. The procedure is painful and could be fatal. On the other hand, if we do nothing, you will surely die for I will not know how to treat you.*

I watched as a thick tube entered my nostril. The initial discomfort turned into searing pain as it entered the geography of the sinus area. I used every tool of meditation to meet and receive the agony. Any flicker towards the past or anticipation of the next moment was way more painful than what was already happening. Like a surfer upon the crest of a great wave, I gave way into a blessed concurrency with the unfolding adventure. There certainly was physical pain, but not the suffering of argument.

As the odyssey continued into the back of my throat, I opened my eyes. The surgeon burst into blinding light before me. Then it happened again. Both nurses were luminous. My body exploded into brightness and a huge wave of the familiar Love swept through me once again!

Here is the challenging part. I am not an "angel kind of guy," and yet the room was congested with Angels! They had settled upon the medical equipment, my bed and everyone present, including me! An upwelling of Great Peace superseded the pain. All I could see were the iridescent light-green wings of The Holy Ones around me. All I could feel was their Love. Divine justice!

During the two ensuing weeks in the hospital, I rested within the grace of Unshakable Love and the radiance of each unfolding moment. Death or life were of no concern. My gratitude and happy heart were more than enough.

THE
BRIDGE
TO
NOWHERE

*D*on't be too quick
    to cross the threshold
from this world
to
the one calling you Home.

You may wish to hesitate
for a moment
before beginning
your Great Adventure.

For the bridge upon which you walk
shall disappear behind you.

And a great unknowingness
will obscure the way ahead.

Listen to the voices of madness
calling you Home.

Come naked into The Mystery.

Toss your garments to the winds.

This is a high path, no railings.

Everything for nothing.

Welcome to the insane asylum.

If deep within you
there lives a devotion to this insanity,
keep walking.

If not, hug tight your clothing.

Return to the land of the sleeping.

You may wish to move swiftly.

Remember,
the bridge is disappearing
behind you.

Oops!

You have probably
crossed the line already.

Here,
hold my hand.

It takes one lunatic
to recognize another.

YOU
WERE
THERE

You were always there,
My Beloved.

Looking back over
corridors of time,
I hear Your invitation moving across
the landscape of my unfolding days,
calling me Home all along.

But I did not have
the ears to hear Your voice.

Upon the fragments
of my broken heart
I smell the fragrance of Your mercy
wafting across my desperation.

But I did not have
the nose to sense Your welcome.

I see Your beckoning smile
awaiting my leap across
Your doorstep.

But I did not have
the eyes to recognize
the glory of Your open door.

I taste Your incredulity
as the carelessness of my words
got me into more trouble
than I remember.

I just did not have
the tongue to savor
Your infinite benevolence.

And
You were there all along,
within every cell
of this blessed body,
dancing in drag as
illness,
sprain,
disease,
cold,
flu,
virus.

I simply did not have
the body to feel You
through the drama of it all.

At last,
My Beloved,
we move together
upon the awakening topography
of my forgetfulness.

Sensuality,
our accompaniment of choice.

These ears,
eyes,
tongue,
nose,
body,
heart
and mind
are Yours now.

The entire catastrophe,
no longer under my jurisdiction.

Here's the joke—
it never was!

Now You get to scratch this head,
smell the roses,
taste the chocolate,
relish the lovemaking
and
praise without ceasing.

Good luck!

You have
the human experience of Gavin.

And I'm out of here!

PETALS
AND
BLOOD

This poem is dedicated to Hafiz*
and his poem "Now Is the Time."

68

*S*educed by the rose,
  pierced by his thorns,
with petals and blood,
Hafiz nailed me.

Now is the time, Gavin,
for you to know
that Everything you do is sacred.

It was the *Everything*
that had me by the balls!

Negotiating my heart
around the enormity of his injunction
didn't work.

I fumbled and fidgeted
until the pain of deflection
was unbearable.

I tried
every practice,
method,
system in the books,
and still a relationship of Sanctity
with *Everything* eluded me.

I railed against the rascal of Shiraz**
hurling my frustration across time.

Disconsolate,
weather-beaten,
trailing blood,
checkmated and defeated,
I gave up.

No idea how to meet
the wild man's challenge.

Searching and seeking
for Sacredness stopped.

And there, My Beloved,
within the heart of that cessation
was a Sacredness beyond describing,
a realization of You,
as *Everything*:
within every expression,
speck,
detail,
facet,
aspect of creation.

Everything shimmering within
Your Glory.

Evolving,
unfolding,
flowering
before my bended knees.

As above, so below,
as The Good Book says.

My Beloved,
 I am willing to make real
the Sacred Gift
within the unfolding
of my life.

I am willing to enter
Your Kingdom upon Earth
with reverence and a fidelity
to what is Real,
True
and utterly Sacred.

And should I feel lost or separated,
I will stop and pour attention
into what is given,
where Everything is considered,
attended
and received as Holy.

To be steadfast,
until the sincerity of my heart
relaxes the sacred moment open,
the way the sun encourages
the macadamia nut blossoms
to release their fragrance
into the early morning light
of North Kohala†.

*See Hafiz's poem Now is the Time, *Appendix 1.*

**Hafiz lived most of his life in Shiraz, Iran.

† Kohala is the name of the northwest portion
of the island of Hawai'i in the Hawaiian Archipelago.

THE ENTIRETY AND THE PARTICULAR

This poem is dedicated to Rumi and his poem "Yesterday At Dawn."

What is your heart's deepest yearning?

What is most important in your life right now?

Is there a One without a second?

What is valued most?

Freedom,
Peace,
Love,
Oneness,
Unity,
Home?

Is there a clarity of intention?

An unshakable resolve?

A non-negotiable aspiration alive within you right now?

Or not?

For
a homesickness within your heart
will be the truest friend
upon your Great Adventure.

Feel the fierce heart of Shams*
beating beside you right now,
overflowing with sincerity—
malleable,
succulent,
tender,
wild.

Give yourself to the intermingling of great hearts longing for Home.

Never blow off the fragrance of those who've blossomed before you.

They may ignite a flowering of your loveliness for all time!

Lean into their words
with a willingness to be changed,
moved
and
perhaps touched forever.

For we are all in this together,
in time and out of time,
and
blossoming is the birthright of us all.

Shams said to Rumi,
*Move with the Entirety
and with the tiniest Particular.*

Turn towards the Entirety.

The Infinite Presence already here,
awaiting the benediction
of your Homecoming.

Give it recognition.

Familiarize yourself
with the vast Field of Awareness
given you.

It is Who You Are.

Shams said,
*Move with the Entirety
and with the tiniest Particular.*

A delicate invitation.

While attending to the Particular
it is easy to lose a sense
of the Entirety,
altogether.

Have you noticed?

Incline attention towards
the Particular and the Entirety.

Both,
together,
simultaneously,
again and again and again,
until dogged familiarity
flowers into a recognition
without ceasing.

The Entirety.

The Particular.

One.

A Divine concurrence.

The Pearl.

*Move with the Entirety
and with the tiniest Particular.*

*Be the moisture in the oyster
that helps to form one Pearl!*

Rumi's teacher was Shams al-Din Mohammad.

See Rumi's poem Yesterday At Dawn, *Appendix 2.*

IN-BETWEEN

*L*et's meet between the known
and
The Unknowable.

Troubled and disturbed
we lie fallow,
naked,
waiting.

All that has been falls away.

Familiarity fades.

We shed our skin.

The ground
beneath us disappears.

We forgive the dream
we cherished.

That life
has outlived its meaning.

We pray without ceasing,
bathing our hearts
in
patience,
incredulity
and bewilderment.

Confounded.

Un-asleep.

Great majesty awaits us.

Something new,
innocent,
fresh,
is flowering.

You!

SMOKE AND MIRRORS

*W*e stand before each other
all smoke, mirrors and mystery.

Two Divine holograms,
reflecting
and refracting
one another's
perfect loveliness
and
imperfect loveliness,
both.

Look!

The hologram is shifting.

I stand before you now
within the glory
of the Absolute Perfection
I Am.

Infinite, aware, whole, empty,
real, true, trustworthy.

As are you,
standing before me,
right now.

The One Great Perfection
flowering as you,
flowering as me
upon the Altar of Truth today.

The hologram shifts again.

Smoke and mirrors come into play.

I stand before you now,
a miracle of relative imperfection
appearing as Gavin,
a human being.

A body, mind, ego, story, personality.

Fallible, changeable
and ultimately imperfect.

As are you, standing before me,
right now.

We are wondrous.

We are Holy.

How amazing!

Let's cast a sacred circle around us,
for we are invited
to a Great Dance together
and the stakes are high.

For until we know
the steps of our dancing,
we shall surely trip
over one another's toes.

Let's stop for a moment,
set aside our dancing shoes
and
pause in prayer before
proceeding across the dance floor.

*May we come to know that
which is utterly Perfect
within ourselves
and*

*recognize the selfsame Perfection
in each other.*

*May we live in devotion
to that Perfection,
fortifying our fidelity
and
connectedness
to the highest of one another.*

*And within this same
holographic dance
may we take great care
with the relative imperfections
of each other,
not as fault but as fact,
abandoning forever
our vainglorious endeavors
to find Perfection
where it is just not possible.*

*That would be like walking
a minefield
or
tiptoeing upon eggshells
as we traverse the dance floor,
wishing for the impossible,
a violence to both of us.*

*Give us the courage, My Beloved,
to step back from our dance
when necessary,
without disconnecting, ever.*

*May we never close
our hearts or our minds
to one another,
even when we keep
a distance between us for a while.*

*Love never means
becoming a doormat.*

*Don't dance
if you don't want to dance.*

*Dragging our disappointments
across the dance floor
is no fun is it?*

*And may you never be caught
within the headlights
of my unwillingness
to see you as you really are.*

Human and Divine, both.

And please return the favor!

So these are our dance steps
my friend.

What's at stake
is peace or war
between us.

Nothing less,
nothing more.

Relatively two.

Absolutely One.

Holograms.

Together.

Now let's get on with dancing!

SLIPPERY
ONE

*F*rom every rooftop I sing
symphonies of love
and adoration for You,
My Beloved.

And each time
I hold You within language
You slide sideways
from my words,
deftly escaping
proximity to my vocabulary.

You are a slippery One.

Even within exalted eloquence,
You will not be captured
nor contained.

And still My Beloved,
when it comes to You,
it's impossible for me
to keep my damn mouth shut.

I can't help myself!

Though I will surely hit a wall
in holy pursuit of the impossible,
I shall venture once again
where even Angels fear to tread.

You are not a guy in the sky
as I was told,
nor a theology,
belief
or anything out there I have to seek,
attain, fear or achieve.

I tried all that
and my wounds are still mending.

You are not a divinely gendered judge
bestowing gold stars
upon deserving foreheads
while casting retribution,
judgment
and punishment upon the wayward,
evil
and those beyond the pale
of spiritual acceptability.

Here I enter the lunatic asylum,
My Beloved.

Will this madness ever end?

You, My Beloved,
are the Empty, Aware Space
into which everything arises
and passes away.

The Conscious Nothingness
that is,
was
and always will be.

The Unknowable,
Primordial,
Unchanging Truth,
already given.

A Timeless Freedom
beyond all these crazy
words and sentences.

The Call of Eternity.

The Infinite Mystery before form.

The Ineffable,
Indestructible,
Groundless Ground.

My Original Face.

The Deathless.

Okay,
enough already!

In the end,
My Beloved,
there is only one thing I do know,
and must say.

Every one of these words,
seemingly directed outwards
towards You,
does a 180° about-turn
and comes back Home
to the Immortal Sacredness
I Am.

Whew!

I have fully dug my grave,
haven't I?

I will shut up now and lie down.

Please start shoveling the dirt!

STEP
INTO MY
BEDROOM

*T*his is how the poems are birthed,
  my friend.

They pull us into the slipstream
of Our Beloved,
where you and I
are seduced into annihilation forever!

In spite of ourselves,
we discover ourselves,
flailing within this web of divinity,
insanity
and madness.

This birth canal knows no shame!

Don't fall asleep.

Be aware.

There are clues
to the seduction everywhere.

Step into my bedroom.

You're welcome to eavesdrop.

This is where the poems
usually begin,
lubricated by the silence of the dark.

Quick,
hide under the covers,
Our Beloved is coming!

Aloha, My Beloved.

I feel the journey of Your hands
moving between the warmth of the sheets,
meandering towards me.

Who needs sleep when
You're cruising the neighborhood.

I am done with dreaming anyway.

Take me, I'm Yours.

Pull me into the shadows with You.

I wonder what exactly
You have in mind for us tonight.

Perhaps You will ravage
and manhandle me again.

I do confess to loving the touch
of Your hand
upon my wrist
as You move the pen
and
pour Your mischief
through my fingertips!

Let's be shameless together
as the moon flirts her way
across the heavens
and
we disappear into the majesty
of Your eloquence forever!

Okay,
you can come out now
my friend!

Please,
take my hand.

This is where you enter the picture
as we tumble
between the lines of this poem
while the words are still warm
and
the portal remains open.

Don't be nervous.

Drop your inhibitions.

Here we are
the Love we have longed for,
in love with each other
and there's nobody here!

Emptiness cavorting
within Emptiness.

And may
the glory of our lovemaking
shatter all vestiges
of self-consciousness,
hurling us
into the fullness of The Vacancy
that we are.

It's so much fun playing with you.

What a divine lover you are,
slipping,
sliding,
dissolving into perpetual mayhem,
forever and ever,
Amen.

True Love, my dear,
Is putting an ironclad grip
Upon the sore swollen balls
Of a Divine Rogue Elephant
And
Not having the good fortune to Die!
—Hafiz

LOVE

For many years, when I was on retreat, I yearned to be as impressively still and angelic as others appeared to be. My experience in meditation was nothing like the peace and calm I anticipated. There was a lot of struggle and striving as I tried to control my emotions and quiet my mind. Occasionally there were fleeting moments when the awareness was simply there, without my effort, but not often. It was tough. Again and again I packed my bags, mobilized to flee in frustration. Each time my heart eventually whispered, *It's all about Love, Gavin. That's why you're here. The doorway to Truth is through the portal of Love. Be kind to yourself. Don't leave!*

The Buddhist Lovingkindness Meditation is not a practice of cultivation. It is a skillful way to jumpstart an upwelling of the Pre-existing Love that lies within all of us. When grappling with the legacy of sexual abuse and the reverberations of my diagnosis, the Lovingkindness Meditation was a great blessing, a benevolent response to the waves of broken-heartedness, fury and self-hatred that blew through from time to time.

Within the storm, a reframing of the classical phrases of Lovingkindness comforted me. By softly repeating the words in meditation, I gently inclined towards the Love I suspected was still there:

May I be happy, just the way I am.
May I be peaceful with all that is occurring, within me and around me.
May I be safe and protected.
May I know ease of well-being within my precious life.
May I love myself completely.

Looking back across my life I realize that Love moved me in ways I neither recognized nor understood at the time. It was all about Love from the very beginning. I just could not recognize the clues nor connect the dots.

Bright orange light filled the room, startling me from sleep. A huge bank of flames was moving up towards the Buddhist Retreat Centre in South Africa where I was living in 1982. I rushed down the mountain and joined hundreds of men, women and children from the surrounding villages. They were already carrying buckets of water to douse the fire. We beat the smoldering grass with wattle branches. We cleared firebreaks. During the night the wind carried clumps of burning grass through the air to distant places. It was a tough battle.

At daybreak the wind subsided and the fire was at last extinguished. Awakening to Love has been a fire, igniting every terrain of lovelessness within me and calling attention to the Love I yearned to know. It took a while to recognize that Love and Awareness are essentially the same. Unconscious love is an oxymoron, altogether impossible. Through the fire of self-acknowledgement, I am wiser, as the flames of Love beautify the places that once scared me. Throwing logs upon that fire is my journey.

Love was never lost, nor did it abandon me. Creative and dynamic like a grass fire, Love is a force of nature. Like fire flying through the air, Love demands expression everywhere. In the end Love trumps everything!

In 1984, when after another long retreat in Massachusetts I returned to South Africa, the "demand of Love" burst forth fiercely. I took long daily walks through the sugar cane fields surrounding the town where my parents lived. My father always discouraged me from entering the plantations. He painted vivid pictures of the malevolence awaiting me within the hills—cane rats, rabid monkeys, pythons and the *drunk and dangerous black men* who lurked about the area.

The winds of Africa whispered sweetly as leaves waved to and fro around me. Each day I took a different route and never knew where I would emerge. All I could see was the path ahead. One day a great noise erupted beside me. The foliage parted and an extremely well-dressed young man, sporting a suit, tie, white shirt and briefcase, crashed through the sugarcane. With a flourish of words I had his life story in minutes, and he mine. His name was Armstrong Zulu. When he heard that I was an accountant, he asked me to help him with his bookkeeping. The students had no teacher at the village school. I invited him to my parent's apartment the next afternoon for our first lesson.

When I told my father, he was outraged, *No! If you give them an inch, they'll take a mile. Don't get involved. You are asking for trouble. What will the neighbors say?* Instead I arranged to work with Armstrong at his school the next day. My father thundered a response, *You can't go to Umgababa Village. It is dangerous. You'll be killed. It's a black area. I forbid it!* He picked up his whisky and fled to the bedroom, disappearing under the

covers. I ripped the sheets from his bed. He was curled up like a baby. Brown terrified eyes looked up at me. I shouted at him for the first and only time in my life, *Never, ever again will you tell me what I can or cannot do!* Early the next morning I left for the Umgababa Village School. I had not been there before. I was scared. I stepped off the train, the only white face in a multitude of early morning commuters, all traveling to work in the white suburbs from which I had come. I was jostled, bumped and pushed. People assumed I was a policeman. No other white folk visited Umgababa Village. Dilapidated dwellings and corrugated iron shanty houses surrounded me as I set off for the school, high up on the mountaintop.

I worked with Armstrong and other students until they left to write their examinations. The headmaster asked me to continue volunteering at the school. Each weekday morning I was joined by chattering schoolchildren and greeted by villagers. For the first time I felt deeply rooted within my beloved country, not an outsider.

At home, the climate was brittle. Every morning I prepared hot cereal, leaving my father's portion on the stove. We did not communicate for weeks. One day I overslept and as I rushed out of the door, he called me back. *Let's have breakfast together and I'll drive you to the school.* He was probably more terrified than I had been as we headed up the dusty mountain track in his beautiful BMW.

The school had neither textbooks nor reading materials, no electricity, telephone or sports equipment. Drinking water was collected from the asbestos roof when it rained. Many students walked over twelve miles without breakfast to school. Children fainted from exhaustion and hunger.

After classes I visited white schools, churches and municipalities. Wherever I went, I asked the same question, *Are you aware that the Umgababa High School has so little, while white schools, surrounded by gardens, swimming pools and tennis courts, are overflowing with books and computers?*

The response was immediate. Truckloads of books, plants and equipment crossed the apartheid divide, ending up on the mountain. My mother's church began a feeding program. Students were given scholarships to an agricultural college. Textbooks were gifted. Money was donated to build four new classrooms.

My mother was in a state of high excitement when I arrived home from school one day. That morning my father had answered the telephone, *This is Mr. Harrison speaking. I believe it is my son you wish to talk to. He is at school. May I help you? Okay. Please give me your address, and I will pick up the books. Thank you. Our children have so much and these Zulu kids have nothing.* He'd fetched the books and surreptitiously included them with others, not mentioning a word about what he had done.

A friend gave money to build shelving for the new school library. I asked my father for advice. He refused. A few days later he offered me a ride to the school again. As we approached the buildings he said: *I think I had better buy the wood and build those shelves. Your efforts will end up being a bloody disaster!* He was probably right. Over the next weeks he built beautiful shelving for thousands of donated books. He and the headmaster became friends. They shared sandwiches and tea each day. He invited Mr. Mgathi and his wife home for dinner, the first time my parents had shared a meal with a black person.

At school we planned a celebration for the opening of the first library in Umgababa Village. All who had helped were invited. The school choir practiced. The children gathered papayas, avocados, sweet potatoes, mangoes, guavas and lichees to give the visitors. On the big day, busloads of white students arrived early in the morning. After an initial moment of discomfort and disorientation, they dissolved into the mass of black students who had gathered to greet them. Apartheid evaporated upon the mountaintop that day. Soon the parking lot was full. The children sang and danced. We planted a tree outside the library. The headmaster, the village chief and a Christian minister all addressed the crowd. As I was saying farewell, I spotted my father standing far away. He was filled with emotion, endeavoring to surreptitiously wipe away the tears that were pouring down his cheeks.

I cherish that memory. For an instant I felt all the contraction and pain of his life.

We had both journeyed a long way to reach the mountaintop. In the end, Love prevailed.

When my father died a few years later, students came to honor him at the memorial service. In lieu of offerings and flowers my mother asked friends to make donations to the Umgababa School.

**REACH
INTO
MY HEART**

*R*each between the folds
    of my grateful heart
and
touch the place that holds you there.

The tenderness you feel
is
the weariness of our hearts,
longing for rest and homecoming.

Separation from Our Beloved
is
the hardest work there is.

The thankfulness you find
is
our relief,
knowing that we are trustworthy to
ourselves
and to a world that holds us closely.

And the softness you meet
is
the benevolence of our hearts
ready to move us
without betrayal or compromise
ever again.

And the tears that fall
caress our weathered hearts,
surrendered humbly,
at last,
into this moment,
without justification or excuse.

One Homesick Heart
coming Home to itself
once and for all.

Now and forever,
Amen.

I'VE
LOOKED
FOR LOVE

I've looked for love
   in all the wrong places.

I have searched for freedom
in worlds of impossibility.

And within
every thwarted
and frustrated endeavor,
My Beloved,
You were there,
nudging,
pushing,
pulling,

seducing
and
pointing me towards Home,
always.

At last,
like a heat-seeking missile,
these eyes have locked upon You
without wavering.

The trajectory of this heart
coming Home to itself,
as You,
is everything now.

The battleground falls silent.

The white flag unfurls
in surrender to Your invitation.

The All that always was,
is
and
will be me,
bows to itself
in welcome and recognition,
and
lays this weary heart
to rest
once and for all.

Raise a fist of freedom
to the sky.

Touch the ground
as the Buddha did.

Seize your birthright.

Let the occupation begin.

Occupy your heart
and let the walls to your Loving
come crumbling down.

Occupy your indignation
that anything less than Liberation
will just not do.

Occupy your willingness
to never forget
who you really, really are,
ever again.

Be true to your heart's
deepest longing.

Lift your voice to the sky
and shout your
True Name
to the heavens above.

Occupy an honesty to this moment,
and move
from the Sacred Ground
of your knowing.

Emancipate your Love
and Be all that
you pray for.

And may this occupation
be the one that ends all occupations,
forever.

Remember the Big Bang,
that great miracle of creation?

Something from nothing?

You are this moment's expression
of that creative force.

Occupy the force of nature
that you are.

And if anyone
messes with your occupation,
set up camp
anywhere and everywhere.

This is where
the rubber hits the road.

Raise your fist.

Open.

Grab the sky.

Touch the ground.

Seize your birthright.

Unfurl great wings.

Occupy all streets everywhere
with your Loving.

OCCUPY
YOUR
HEART

FRODO AND SAM

*This poem is dedicated to Frodo and Sam,
two dogs that have blessed my life.*

We are devotees of the night.

And while
Our Beloved adorns the evening sky
with the Majesty of Heaven,
I freefall into Love again
as we tumble through the stars
together.

I bow before the Love you are.

I am in devotion
to your devotion to me.

You are magicians of Love,
as molecule for molecule
you match and multiply
the Love you receive.

This is no ordinary Love affair.

Your liquid eyes sparkle
with adoration?

All I see is You,
My Beloved,
loving me.

Your funny ears sensing the galaxies,
listening for the music of the stars?

All I feel is Your anticipation
My Beloved,
awaiting the footfalls
of my Homecoming.

That wagging tail
betrays Your happiness
that
I am Homeward bound.

I wag my tail in solidarity.

Eyes ablaze,
ears in ecstatic salute,
drooling as if there's no tomorrow,
or yesterday either,
here we are,
barking in Timeless Love together.

It doesn't get any better than this!

A HANDFUL
OF
STARS

I return you to the stars
  from whence you came.

While Our Beloved
casts handfuls of diamonds
across the African sky in celebration.

At last I allow you
to be exactly who you are.

Emancipated from my judgment.

Liberated from my expectations.

No longer flailing within
my wishes and hopes for you,
you get to be
the Angel you are.

And within your slipstream,
so do I.

The Milky Way
reaches down and blesses us.

The heavens above Grootbos*
glitter in welcome
as all the stars of this life
return to the galaxies
from which they came.

Whole.

Unscathed in the end.

Beautiful beyond describing.

Please,
take my hand and join the festivities
as we cruise the cosmos together,
catch the falling stars around us,
play among the planets
and
head for the moon together!

*"Grootbos" is an Afrikaans word meaning "big bush," an
ecological area in the Western Cape of South Africa where
the mountainsides are home to 650 related plant species,
including proteas and pincushions.

A NEW DAY

*M**ay* a kaleidoscope of possibilities
greet you
upon the threshold of this new day.

May all that is utterly innocent,
new,
vulnerable and true
find its way between
the fluttering of your eyelashes
as they open to the
immeasurable glory around you.

May your heart release its gift
before thought and self-involvement
obscure
the limitless possibilities ahead.

And may this daybreak
midwife footsteps
unfettered by habit and repetition.

May you follow the thread of Love
winding outward from the silence
of your awakening heart
into the majesty of a world
anticipating your loveliness.

And within the unfolding
of this sacred day,
may you remember,
without forgetting,
the infinite blessing that you are
as you step into
The Mystery of A New Day.

I am happy even before I have a reason.
                                    —*Hafiz*

GRATITUDE

During the winter of 1973, many students at the English-speaking colleges in South Africa protested the inequality between black and white education under apartheid. Late one night, six of us sat huddled together, holding our placards, on the pavement of Jan Smuts Avenue beside the campus of The University of the Witwatersrand, in Johannesburg. It was cold. Rush-hour traffic to the affluent white suburbs in the north was long over. The daily exodus to Soweto and Alexandria Township was also complete. Passersby were rarely friendly. To our delight, a car stopped and a woman handed us a plate of homemade pies. A friend suggested that we inspect the pastries before eating them. In the beam of the flashlight, tiny pieces of glass glittered within the meat.

A few days later, during a large demonstration, police vans from John Vorster Square pulled up in front of us. Traffic was halted. Hundreds of policemen wielding truncheons, gas masks and weapons, lined up before us. They bristled with anticipation and obviously relished the possibilities ahead. A whistle blew. Within moments our campus was a war zone. Beaten up, dragged by the hair, eyes blinded by the gas, I could not stop crying. I was exhausted, done with a life of coping, fighting and surviving. After graduating I left South Africa, accompanied by my partner of several years.

He and I had triumphed over much. We'd met in 1971 in Johannesburg. We were both in relationships with women and double-dated for a while. At discotheques in Johannesburg we held hands under the table and danced as close to each other as we could. Soon the sexual attraction between us trumped the façade. We survived a hostile environment antagonistic to our sexuality and overcame the attempts of our parents to separate us.

We traveled in Europe for a year before settling in Iran, one of the few countries in the world where white South Africans could legally live and work at that time. Penniless, we began the final chapter of our relationship.

We lived in downtown Tehran, a far cry from the affluence surrounding the Shah's Palace on the foothills of the Alborz Mountains above the city. I spoke Farsi and felt welcomed into the local neighborhood. We explored ancient archaeological sites around the country. In the springtime we picnicked under cherry blossom trees beside streams of melting snow. Unbeknownst to us, the threads of my early abuse were interwoven into the tapestry of our relationship. In 1978 I succumbed to a deeply instinctual and confounding resistance to our intimacy. I loved him and rejected him at the beginning of the Iranian uprising, a revolution that later endangered his life and killed many of his students. As I flailed within the enveloping darkness and confusion of this time, My Beloved reached out to me, at a gathering of friends, one cold and icy night, in a beautiful home on the outskirts of the city.

The fragrances from our feasting followed us into the living room: rich pomegranate and walnut from the khoresh fesenjan chicken stew, golden buttery Shirazi rice-polow flavored with cinnamon, nutmeg, cumin and saffron, and Caspian eggplant braise redolent with turmeric, garlic, honey, parsley and cilantro. And oh, the desserts from Yazd! At 12,000 feet, its pastries are the finest, most delicate and subtly flavored in Iran, especially the sanbuseh we ate, overflowing with almonds, pistachios, cardamom and rosewater.

We sat in a circle together, our legs draped in rugs and our toes reaching towards the warmth of the covered coals in the center. Layers of Persian carpets and cushions softened the ground beneath us. Silk tapestries adorned the walls, their gold thread and freshwater pearls catching the light from time to time.

Outside, heavy snow blanketed Teheran. Inside, the sound of the santoor—an ancient stringed musical instrument native to Persia—entered our silence. And then the poetry began. Waves of emotion swept through the room. Tears began falling. The language, I did not fully understand. It was old, not the modern colloquial Farsi I knew. Men who were uncommunicative and withdrawn at the dinner table sobbed openly as sacred words began weaving a web of reverence, devotion and love around me. A friend whispered, *Hafiz, Hafiz, Hafiz*. My tears joined those of others.

For an instant I glimpsed an open doorway beckoning me with an invitation I was not yet ready to accept.

A few months later I gazed across the desert sands as my flight landed in Shiraz, a cultured and beautiful city that had escaped the violence and destruction of the Mongol and Tartar invasions. I stepped out of the plane into a world of perfume and color. Shiraz is the City of Roses. Its rosewaters have flowed out to the world for countless centuries. Yet infinitely more beautiful is the fragrance of the Great Flower of Shiraz, wafting across eight centuries and gracing our world with Timeless Wisdom and Love: *Hafiz, Hafiz, Hafiz!*

Perhaps I strolled down the same streets he had walked. I joined generations of pilgrims at his tomb in the beautiful Musalla Gardens, adorned with citrus orchards, ponds, flowing streams, flowers, pathways and of course roses.

Today I know, without doubt, that My Beloved has been holding my hand and tending my heart throughout my life, every step of the way, particularly within my darkest hours. I never did leave my magic garden, ever. I simply did not recognize that it was there, waiting, all along.

ANCHOR

Y*ou* did it again, My Beloved.

Summoning me from dreamtime,
naked and shivering,
into the full-moon light.

Great white owls
crisscrossed the sky,
casting long shadows
into
the perfect loveliness of the night.

An assembly of pigs parted
the grass before us
as
You dislodged the anchor
dropped into this fleeting world
long, long ago.

I breathed
a forgotten breath once again.

The winds of Waipio*
hurled clouds
across the heavens above.

Showers from Pololu* inducted me
into The Mysteries,
anointing my head
with moonbeams and raindrops,
scattering a million gems
upon a sacred moment,
sanctifying our togetherness
and
blessing the holy ground
of North Kohala.

Sing Your Songs through me.

I will move to Your melody
as no one has before.

Anchorless,
untethered,
I am Yours,
forever and ever,
Amen.

*Hawai‘i's Waipio Valley is the first of five sacred valleys that stretch along the coast of the Kohala Mountain to Pololu.

ACROSS
THE VELD

I have cast myself to the ground
more times than I can remember,
My Beloved.

For flat upon my face
I feel the roar of Africa within me
as benediction,
blessing
and privilege.

Mother Africa,
tear asunder
all inhibition to the Love
that lives here now.

May I move
as your humble child
wherever the currents of Your will
might catapult me into this world.

For I am of this ground,
and my roots run wild and deep
within You.

This is my prayer:

Mother Africa,
dignify me with Your stature,
infuse me with Your resilience,
and grace me with Your strength.

May I be a clear voice
and an empty vessel for Your Love.

For across the veld* of this weary life,
the dust is settling
and the fog is lifting.

Every landscape of forgetfulness
prepared me for this moment
of remembrance
and annihilation.

Every wrong turn,
a leap towards You.

Every struggle,
a doorway to the end of struggle.

This African mind
sinks into a humbled heart.

That mind was never mine anyway.

Mother Africa,
You have returned me to myself
at last.

I am grateful beyond measuring.

I am The Beloved
My Beloved promised I would be.

I am all I yearned for,
and so much more,
and less.

Everything and nothing.

Filled and empty.

I Am, My Beloved.

I simply Am.

And may God Bless Africa,
and everyone,
everywhere.

*Veld is an Afrikaans word for the
savanna or the grasslands.

A TALL STORY

A star crosses the night sky,
  receding silently
into the next galaxy,
dragging the debris,
drama
and disappointments
of a lifetime in its wake.

The adventure continues,
the protagonist is toast!

The center has fallen
from a narration
that was never mine anyway.

I have lost all interest in stories
and storytelling.

Mine is no longer sticky
and I can't stick to the story
any longer.

As soap operas go
the saga of Gavin was a good one.

Drama queens
make for great entertainment!

Now I'm no longer resident
within a tall tale I once told.

I cannot get it up for romances,
thrillers
and
cliffhangers any longer,
mine or yours.

I have lost all interest
in your story as well.

Sorry!

Let's rather meet on
Holy Ground,
without narrative.

It is a forgiving place,
having put up with this sleepwalker
and
yarn spinner for so long.

Here your story disappears also
and
the resplendency
of who you Truly are
supersedes all fiction.

Unbound
and unboxed,
let's bow in ecstatic devotion
to that which is greater
than any bestseller could ever be.

Amen.

IT'S
JUST
AS WELL

It is just as well I did not know
how much You wanted me,
My Beloved.

For I would have fled,
panic stricken,
before the prospect of that intimacy.

It is just as well I did not know
how unforgiving Your demand
for self-honesty would be.

For the fire of that injunction
would have been way too hot
for me to handle.

It is just as well I did not know
how many lines
You would have me cross.

For I would have gripped
my prison bars more tightly
in terror
than ever before.

It is just as well I did not know
how absolute Your need
for all of my humanity would be.

For the thought of inhabiting
every part of my humanness
would have catapulted me
deeper than ever
into contraction and hiding.

It is just as well I did not know
how seamless
my fidelity to You
would turn out to be.

For I would have exited,
howling and screaming,
before the magnitude
of that commitment.

It is just as well I did not know
how much Love
You would pour into this life.

For I would have drowned
within the intimations
of all that Glory and Vulnerability.

And it is just as well I did not know
how simple and ordinary
this that I Am
would turn out to be.

For
the specialness and grandiosity
that once lived here
would have had nothing to do
with The Quietude and Emptiness
that is here now.

And so,
My Beloved,
it is just as well.

IN THE END

*I*n the end
there is only one prayer.

Help me see the Truth.

And once only.

Thereafter the mind weaves words
into a tapestry of its own design
and true prayer is lost.

Bringing the language of earth
to the secrets of Heaven
is a delicate and tender endeavor.

In the end
there's only one longing.

Follow that thread
all the way Home.

Give way
into the Homesickness
of your longing heart.

You have every reason to do so.

In the end there is only one Love.

It does not come,
it does not go.

This Love is who you are.

Abiding and beyond describing.

Why settle for less?

In the end
there's only one thing to do.

Nothing.

Stop,
show up,
wait,
receive,
listen for the next step,
bow before what is given.

vDon't do anything.

More is a movement from The Truth.

And only The Truth
will set you free.

In the end
there is only one surrender.

Everything.

Nowhere to go.

You are already there.

NO
CREATED
THING

*K*nown now
is The Sacred Ground
to which no created thing can go.

A Great Silence
into which the sounds of creation
appear and disappear.

A Timeless Place
where future and past
have no meaning.

A Vast Emptiness
within which the story of Gavin
constellates and evaporates.

A Compassion,
ceaselessly responsive
to the suffering of all created beings.

Unboundaried,
Unconfined,
Unfathomable.

A Peace that Passeth all Understanding,
wherein
the glories and consternations of creation
arise and pass away.

A Love
way beyond
the limitation of language,
altogether.

A Oneness
where division,
difference
and distinction are impossible.

And should I root within created things,
My Beloved
swiftly defaults me right back
to the Sacred Ground
I know myself to be.

And that gap is closing.

APPENDICES

NOW IS THE TIME

by Hafiz
Translated by Daniel Ladinsky

Now is the time to know
That all that you do is sacred.

Now, why not consider
A lasting truce with yourself and God.

Now is the time to understand
That all your ideas of right and wrong
Were just a child's training wheels
To be laid aside
When you finally live
With veracity
And love.

Hafiz is a divine envoy
Whom the Beloved
Has written a holy message upon.

My dear, please tell me,
Why do you still
Throw sticks at your heart
And God?

What is it in that sweet voice inside
That incites you to fear?

Now is the time for the world to know
That every thought and action is sacred.

This is the time
For you to compute the impossibility
That there is anything
But Grace.

Now is the season to know
That everything you do
Is sacred.

YESTERDAY AT DAWN

by Rumi
Translated by Coleman Barks

Yesterday at dawn, my Friend said,
How long will this unconsciousness go on?

You fill yourself with the sharp pain of Love,
rather than its fulfillment.

I said:
"But I can't get to You!
You are the whole dark night,
and I am a single candle.

My life is upside down because of You!"

The Friend replied,
I am your deepest being.
Quit talking about wanting me!

I said,
"Then what is this restlessness?"

The Friend:
Does a drop stay still in the Ocean?
Move with the Entirety and with the tiniest Particular.
Be the moisture in an oyster that helps to form one pearl.

WOZA MOYA

IXOPO WWW.WOZAMOYA.ORG.ZA

The Woza Moya Project runs a community-care and support program in the Ofafa Valley, about fifteen kilometers from the town of Ixopo in KwaZulu-Natal, South Africa. The Project began in April 2000 as a community-based response to the devastating impact of HIV and AIDS. It is a vast hilly region, with almost no electricity, telecommunications or sanitation. One 30 km road winds its way through the area.

The Ofafa area is home to about 23,000 people. It is a community seriously affected by HIV, AIDS, poverty and a lack of resources. Recent statistics reveal that 47% of the pregnant women presenting themselves at the prenatal clinic in Ixopo are HIV positive. Of general patients referred for voluntary counseling and HIV testing in a five-month period, 78% tested positive. The vision of the Woza Moya Project is that each child, woman and man in the Ofafa Valley community will have the medical and social support, food security, education and resources they need to overcome the impact of HIV and tuberculosis in their lives.

The Woza Moya Project currently has a staff of twenty, supplemented by thirty community-based care-workers, serving upwards of 8,000 people, providing home-based care, food security, emotional support, paralegal services, early childhood development programs at the on-site play center and water, sanitation and hygiene interventions. The Woza Moya Project is widely respected throughout South Africa, where it is considered a model community response to the HIV and AIDS pandemic in Africa.

For seven years the Hawai'i Meditation Community has partnered with the Woza Moya Project to provide funding and support. For information about the Woza Moya–Hawai'i Community Fundraising Project, visit gavinharrison.net.

GROUP OF HOPE

cohesion leads
to victory

GROUP OF HOPE

The Group of Hope has been underway since 2002 and has survived to challenge all attempts to shut it down. This unique, prisoner-initiated program, begun in Brandvlei Prison, a maximum-security facility near Worcester in the Western Cape, offers the only alternative to joining the notorious prison gang system in South Africa. The group continues to challenge everyone's perceptions about prisoners. In the end, the program is not just about the people in the Group, for the membership changes as inmates join and some are eventually released back into their communities; it is about the transformative power of hope and love in lives not accustomed to such possibilities.

The men of the Group of Hope have adopted many orphaned and vulnerable children from the surrounding townships.

They raise money to help feed, clothe and keep these children in school by making jewelry out of recycled paper. As one group member says, *I am not just rolling paper beads, I am rolling opportunities for our orphans. Each and every bead contains them.* The children regularly visit their unlikely benefactors and the bond between them has transformed both sets of lives.

The Group of Hope inmates also run HIV prevention campaigns within the prison, as well as workshops for troubled youths from the community.

For further information about the Group of Hope visit groupofhope.co.za and mothersforall.org.

PHOTOGRAPHERS

The images within this book have been used with the permission of the photographers below.
Unacknowledged photographs were taken by Gavin.

CATHERINE ANDERSON Charlotte, North Carolina, USA. www.catherineandersonstudio.com

CARLOS EYLES Kailua Kona, Hawai'i, USA. www.carloseyles.com

THERESE COOPER Pretoria, South Africa. slowveld@hotmail.co.za

ii 8 12 38 50 54 60 83
86 94 108 110

WENDY WAGNER Kapaau, Hawaiʻi, USA. wwagner7@gmail.com

i/vi /68 iv viii 2 4 16 18
22 25 26 28 30 32 40 44
58 49 62 64 74 79 81 92
98 104 112 114

DESIGN AND LAYOUT

Tim Dubitsky is a visual artist and designer who retired to Hawai'i in 2011 at the age of thirty-three. A fan of beautiful things, he eschewed his retirement status to work on *Petals and Blood*. Hawi, Hawai'i, USA. tedubitsky@gmail.com

PERMISSIONS

Hafiz poems and excerpts are from the following Penguin publications and used with author's permission:

I Heard God Laughing by Daniel Ladinsky.
Copyright © 1996 & 2006 Daniel Ladinsky.

The Gift: Poems by Hafiz by Daniel Ladinsky.
Copyright © 1999 Daniel Ladinsky.

The Subject Tonight is Love: 60 Wild and Sweet Poems of Hafiz by Daniel Ladinsky.
Copyright © 1996 & 2003 Daniel Ladinsky.

Rumi poems and excerpts are from the following publications and used with author's permission:

The Essential Rumi by Coleman Barks, published by HarperCollins.
Copyright © 1995 Coleman Barks.

The Book of Love: Poems of Ecstasy and Longing by Coleman Barks, published by HarperCollins.
Copyright © 2003 Coleman Barks.

The Illuminated Rumi by Coleman Barks, published by Broadway Books.
Copyright © 1997 Coleman Barks.